Mendocino Coast Cooking

Recipes from Restaurants, Bed & Breakfast Inns
and Culinary Resources
on the Mendocino Coast of California

Compiled and Edited by Gail Levene

Photography by Mara Levene

Illustrations by Jane Russell

Pacific Transcriptions
Mendocino, California

Copyright © 1999
by
Pacific Transcriptions
P.O. Box 526   Mendocino, CA. 95460
(707) 937-4801   pactrans@mcn.org

Library of Congress Catalog Number: 86-60038
ISBN Number: 0-933391-06-4

Manufactured in the United States of America

The recipes in this book have been received directly from the contributors and printed with their permission. Some recipes and other materials were previously printed in Mendocino Cookery, Mendocino Coast Cooking, *and* Mendocino Wines & Cooking, *all published by Pacific Transcriptions.*
Navarro Oysters, *and* Wakame, Cabbage and Bean Thread, *by Eleanor Lewallen, are reprinted, by permission, from* Sea Vegetable Gourmet Cookbook, © 1983 by Mendocino Sea Vegetable Company, Navarro, Ca.

The front cover photograph, inside the Platt House at Todd's Point, is by Leona Walden.

The back cover photograph, of the Salmon Barbecue, Noyo, is by Rick Browne © 1997. The cooks are Patty Campbell of Fort Bragg and Bill Townsend of Ukiah. Thanks to Cammie Conlon and the Fort Bragg-Mendocino Coast Chamber of Commerce for permission to use this photograph.

Thanks to Judy Tarbell and Black Bear Press for their help and encouragement.

Photograph Locations

Page 1—Gualala
Page 2—Mendocino
Page 6—Elk
Page 8—Fort Bragg
Page 23—Little River
Page 24—Westport
Page 30—Mendocino
Page 40—Mendocino
Page 47—Caspar
Page 48—Point Arena
Page 58—Little River

Page 64—Mendocino
Page 75—Gualala
Page 76—Elk
Page 82—Albion
Page 90—Noyo
Page 107—Mendocino
Page 108—Manchester
Page 131—Fort Bragg
Page 132—Comptche
Page 140—Fort Bragg

Contents

Introduction

This is a collection of recipes used by restaurants, bed & breakfast inns and culinary resources on the Mendocino Coast of Northern California. Although many of these recipes were developed or adapted here, there does not exist, specifically, a 'Northern California Regional Cooking.' Many (but not all—some are unique) of the recipes were derived from those used in other parts of the world. Accordingly, foods eaten on the Mendocino Coast are truly diverse, reflecting the ethnic backgrounds of their creators. A cursory examination shows 20 distinct origins: African, Caribbean, Chinese, Creole, Dutch, French, German, Greek, Irish, Italian, Jewish, Mexican, Russian, Scandinavian, Scottish, 'Southern,' Thai, Viennese, and Vietnamese—a distinctly international flavor, but naturally many of the recipes are as American as apple pie.

Pleasurable as it has been compiling this book, greater enjoyments are to be had in preparing the foods and possibly visiting, or ordering from, the contributors. It is the author's hope that many will partake of those pleasures and this book is dedicated to all who enjoy good food.

Appetizers,
Condiments,
&
Sauces

The MacCallum House Restaurant
and Grey Whale Bar & Cafe of Mendocino

Chef Alan Kantor's

Gnocchi with Walnut-Arugula Pesto and melted Cambozola Cheese

Gnocchi

> **2 pounds russet potatoes**
>
> **3 egg yolks**
>
> **1 1/2 cups all-purpose flour**
>
> **1/2 tablespoon salt**

Bake the potatoes until soft (well-done). When the potatoes are done, put on a large pot of salted water and bring to a boil. Peel and rice the potatoes while warm. To rice, pass the potato through a ricer or food mill. Add the rest of the ingredients and knead until it becomes a smooth dough. Divide the dough into 4-6 pieces and, on a lightly floured surface, roll into logs about 1/2 inch wide. Cut diagonally into pieces 1/2 to 3/4 inch long. Roll the pieces off a fork into the boiling water. When gnocchi come back to the surface they are ready.

To serve immediately, take them out and put them directly into the pesto. To prepare ahead, take gnocchi out of the water and place them on a towel-lined sheet pan and refrigerate. To re-heat, immerse in boiling water until they float to the surface again.

Recipe will make 10 appetizers or 5 large portions.

Walnut-Arugula Pesto

> **1/2 cup water**
>
> **2 bunches arugula**
>
> **2 large cloves of garlic**
>
> **1 ounce red wine vinegar**
>
> **1/2 cup grated dry Jack, Parmesan or Romano cheese**
>
> **1/2 cup extra virgin olive oil**
>
> **1/2 cup toasted walnuts (bake for 10 minutes at 350°)**

Place the water in the bottom of a blender. De-stem arugula and place in blender (save some for garnish). Add the rest of the ingredients to the blender and blend until smooth.

In a pan, heat 1 tablespoon pesto and 1 tablespoon heavy cream through. Add about 12 hot gnocchi (just made or re-heated) per person. Add a pinch of salt to taste. Toss the gnocchis in the pesto to coat and place on plates with a thin slice of Cambozola cheese on top. Garnish with a little arugula, walnut, and red pepper & yellow pepper confetti.

Sea Rock Bed & Breakfast Inn of Mendocino

Great Guacamole

4 ripe avocados

1 lemon

2 ripe tomatoes, chopped

1 fresh jalapeño pepper, very finely chopped

1/8 cup white onion, finely chopped

1 cup small curd cottage cheese

1 teaspoon Worcestershire sauce

4 (or) 5 dashes Tabasco sauce

Peel and slice each avocado into 4 to 6 thick slices. In a large bowl mash the avocado slices with a potato masher or fork (Don't mash avocados into a pulp—leave some chunks).

Add: the juice from the lemon—stirring, so lemon juice contacts all the avocado (lemon juice will keep the avocado green).

Add: 2 chopped tomatoes, 1 cup cottage cheese, 1 very finely chopped jalapeño pepper, 1/8 cup finely chopped white onion, 1 teaspoon Worcestershire sauce, and 4 to 5 dashes Tabasco sauce.

Mix ingredients.

Then, chill 15-20 minutes.

Then serve with corn chips, etc.

Mendocino Sea Vegetable Company of Navarro

Navarro Oysters

'Navarro Oysters' are a real hit as an appetizer on social occasions, or as a dinner treat. When we serve them at fairs, people come back for more again and again! We call them 'Navarro Oysters' because this recipe was created in a historic redwood house in Navarro, California, and they resemble deep-fried oysters in flavor-only better. And even if you don't like oysters, you'll like these.

> **1 cup or 1 ounce dried nori**
> **1/4 cup whole wheat flour**
> **1/4 teaspoon baking soda**
> **1 egg**
> **1/2 cup mllk (or water)**
> **1 to 2 tablespoons soy sauce (to taste)**
> **hot sauce, to taste**
> **1 onion, diced**
> **2/3 cup safflower or other cooking oil**

Combine flour and baking soda, add milk and egg (egg can be omitted if desired); add soy sauce and hot sauce. Mix this batter. Break nori into small pieces, and stir the pieces into the batter. The nori will absorb moisture in the batter as you cut and add the onion. This batter is basically a thin pancake batter; but as nori absorbs moisture and flavor, the mixture becomes a gooey mass. Fear not.

To fry, pick out with chopsticks, fork or fingers small amounts, and deep fry 2 or 3 pieces at a time in hot oil until golden brown and crisp on both sides. Remove with chopsticks or forks, drain, and serve immediately, as an appetizer (serves eight), or as a main dish with rice (serves four).

Liptauer Dip

In a large mixer bowl combine the following:

    1 1/4 pints large curd cottage cheese
    2 tablespoons Hungarian Paprika
    2 teaspoons salt
    1 teaspoon pepper
    1 1/2 teaspoons Colman's Dry Mustard
    6 tablespoons finely chopped green onions
    8 anchovy filets, WELL drained and finely chopped
    2 cloves garlic, minced
    1/4 cup capers, drained

Add:

    1/2 pound butter, softened
    12 ounces cream cheese, softened

Add and Mix:

    1 cup sour cream
    3 tablespoons caraway seed

Chill overnight. Will keep refrigerated 1 week.

Howard Creek Ranch Inn of Westport

Pacific Crab Dip

1/3 to 1/2 pound of crab, shredded
1 cup mayonnaise
1/4 carrot, finely chopped
1/2 cup celery
1/2 bunch green onions
1/4 cup onions
1 can cream of mushroom soup
1 8-ounce package cream cheese
1 1/2 packages gelatin

Combine crab, mayonnaise, carrots, celery, and onions.
Heat and melt together musroom soup, cream cheese and gelatin.
Combine all ingredients and refrigerate.
Serve with crackers or tortilla chips.

RoundMan's SmokeHouse of Fort Bragg

Smoked Salmon Spread

8 ounces cream cheese
1 bunch green onions
1 flat can chopped olives
4-8 ounces RoundMan's Smoked Salmon
1-2 teaspoons dry dill (optional)
chopped parsley (optional)

Soften cream cheese, finely chop green onions. Break up Salmon, check for and discard any bones. Mix all ingredients thoroughly. Chill. Roll in chopped parsley if desired.

Variation: 1 dozen 12" flour tortillas. Spread salmon spread on flour tortillas. Roll up and chill for 2 hours. Cut into 1/2" slices and arrange on plate for tasty and pretty hors d'oeuvres.

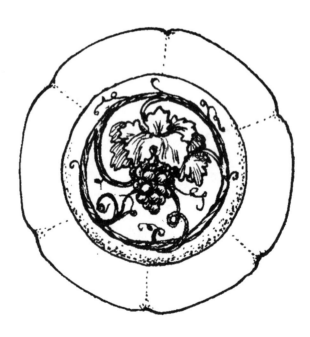

Mendocino Farmers' Market

Judy Summers'
Garlic & Herb Cream Cheese

8 ounces cream cheese

2-3 tablespoons milk

2-3 cloves garlic

1/4 cup chives, chopped fine

1/8 cup parsley, chopped fine

pinch dried thyme

salt & pepper to taste

Beat cream cheese, gradually adding milk to thin it somewhat. It should be light and fluffy, not soupy. Add garlic, chives, parsley, thyme, salt, and pepper. Mix with spoon. Taste for seasoning.

Serve on crackers, toast, or use as a filling for omelet. Also good on toasted bagels.

Mendocino Mustard
(Hand-prepared on the Mendocino Coast since 1977)

Peanut Mustard Sauce

A Thai-inspired sauce for snapper, cod, tuna or halibut fillets. Also great on tofu or as a stir-fry sauce.

Ingredients:

1 cup pineapple juice

1/4 cup peanut butter

2 cloves garlic, minced

2 teaspoons soy sauce

4 tablspoons Hot & Sweet Mendocino Mustard

Directions:

Combine pineapple juice, peanut butter, garlic and soy sauce in a sauce pan. Bring to a boil, reduce heat, add mustard. Cook until thickened. Cool to room temperature or refrigerate until ready to use.

Spread sauce on uncooked fillets and arrange in a buttered baking dish. Bake in a preheated 375° oven for 5 to 10 minutes or until fish is cooked.

Bonus:

Peanut Mustard Sauce is also terrific with barbequed hot dogs or sausages.

Grebiche Sauce
for Chilled Asparagus or Fish

(Also great on sandwiches!)

2 tablespoons Dijon mustard

1 shallot

1 garlic clove

2 egg yolks

1 tablespoon lemon juice (could be more if lemons are not acidic)

1 teaspoon tarragon

1 tablespoon capers

1 sweet comichon pickles

3/4 cup peanut oil

1/4 cup olive oil

salt & cayenne to taste

Process first 8 ingredients together well (at least 1 minute), and then slowly add the oils.

Season to taste.

If sauce is too thick, thin with water or brandy.

Good Thyme Herb Blends of Mendocino

Debra Dawson's
A Sauce For Any Vegetable

A sauce for any vegetable cooked in water can be made as follows:

Use only a minimum of water, with salt and/or any herb you like, in a heavy-bottomed pot sized for the quantity you're cooking. After some evaporation during boiling you should have about a cup left; this bouillon contains the flavor of your vegetable and any vitamins which may survive. Cook only until tender-don't overcook. Those pieces not actually in the water will be steamed, and you may gently stir or toss once or twice while cooking. Drain and reserve the liquid.

Put as much butter as you would have put anyway on your vegetable, back into the empty pot on medium heat. Melt and add an equal quantity of flour to make a roux blanc. As you cook the roux, slowly add the liquid from your vegetables, whisking to prevent lumps. As it thickens, add more bouillon but don't make it too thin. Cook 7-10 minutes, or more if you have time. A little cream or milk will make it whiter and richer. Replace the vegetables and gently re-warm 5 minutes. Garnish with chopped parsley, chives or cilantro.

Assuming you were going to use butter, this makes an elegant side dish for any vegetable while adding only a little flour. It uses what would be lost in the cooking liquid, is entirely vegetarian and naturally the sauce is harmonious with the vegetable. The addition of grated cheese makes this into a light cheese sauce.

Appetizers, Condiments, & Sauces

Blue's Cafe at Caspar Inn

Chef Jude Henderson's
"Boogie Pig's Pink Tartar"

1 cup whole egg mayonaise
1 cup good quality ketchup
1 cup sweet relish and its juice
1/2 teaspoon tabasco
juice of one ripe lemon
1 tablespoon sundried tomatoes, softened
1/2 minced yellow onion
3 cloves fresh garlic, minced

In a large bowl, add all ingredients. With a whisk, whip vigorously to smooth and fluffy. Makes 3 cups.

Store in refrigerator. Has shelf life of 1 week.

At the Blue's Cafe, this sauce accompanies our battered cod and chip basket, and is also used on our grilled Cajun breast of chicken sandwich!

Heritage House of Little River

Walnut Plum Relish

2 cups plum puree

1/2 cup sugar

3 cinnamon sticks

3 tablespoons rice wine vinegar

2 tablespoons water

1/2 cup skinned, chopped walnuts

4 cloves

1/4 cup good plum liquor

Simmer half an hour. Remove cinnamon and cloves.
Serve with pork.

Mendocino Mineral Water of Comptche

A few ideas using the mineral water other than drinking it straight:

When preparing frozen juices, use the plain mineral water instead of tap water for an extra healthy, sparkling drink.

Or you could choose one of the flavored waters—lime, orange, lemon, or strawberry—to mix with a complimentary flavored juice.

The lemon and lime mineral waters mix especially well with wine for a sparkling wine cooler or wine punch.

One way we have discovered to use the plain mineral water in cooking is to substitute the water in your favorite waffle recipe for fluffier waffles.

Breads,
Tea Breads,
Coffee Cakes
&
Breakfasts

Cafe Beaujolais of Mendocino

Cornmeal Cream Biscuits

1 1/2 teaspoons white sugar

1 1/3 cup white flour, unsifted

2/3 cup cornmeal

1 tablespoon baking powder

3/4 teaspoon salt

1/4 cup unsalted butter,
>   cut into 1/2 teaspoon-sized pieces & frozen

1 cup + 2 tablespoons heavy cream

Mix dry ingredients together. Add butter and blend briskly with your fingertips, rubbing the dry ingredients with the butter until butter is broken up into smaller pieces (about the size of peas). Add heavy cream and using a fork, combine all ingredients until just moistened. Immediately turn out onto a lightly-floured board and knead ten times ONLY. It's okay if small lumps of butter are visible.

Roll out to 3/4-inch thick and cut with a floured cutter, 2-inches in diameter, as close together as possible to minimize re-rolling OR make square biscuits. Layer the leftover bits and pieces and knead two or three times, pat out dough again and cut biscuits.

Place biscuits on a 10"x15"x1" ungreased cookie sheet and bake at 425° for 15 to 18 minutes or until golden brown.

Makes 10-12.

Serenisea Ocean Cabins of Gualala

Marcia Lotter's
Serenisea Potato Biscuits

1 package yeast
1/2 cup sugar
3/4 cup butter, melted
1 cup milk, scalded
2 cups mashed potatoes, sieved
2 eggs
1 teaspoon salt
unbleached flour

Make a batter of all ingredients with only enough flour to thicken. Let rise for 1 hour. Add enough flour to make soft dough and let rise another hour. Roll out and cut like biscuits (about 1/4-inch thick). Layer two of these for each biscuit and let rise a third hour before baking at 370° for about 20 minutes.

The Pudding Creek Inn of Fort Bragg

Old-Fashioned Rhubarb Muffins

2 1/2 cups regular flour

2/3 cup granulated sugar

3 teaspoons baking powder

1/2 teaspoon salt

1 cup milk

1/4 cup vegetable oil

1/2 to 3/4 teaspoon vanilla extract

1 egg, beaten

2 cups fresh rhubarb, finely chopped

1/2 cup nuts, chopped,
>   for sprinkling over the muffin tops prior to baking (optional)

Place chopped rhubarb in a medium bowl and toss with 1 to 2 teaspoons regular sugar. Set aside.

In large bowl combine flour, salt, 2/3 cup regular sugar and baking powder.

Using a third bowl, combine milk, oil, vanilla and beaten egg. Add this liquid all at once to the large bowl of dry ingredients—stir gently with a wooden spoon just until moistened. Carefully and lightly fold the rhubarb into the batter. Spoon batter into greased muffin pans, filling about 2/3 full. Bake at 400 degrees for 20-25 minutes or till top springs back when lightly pressed. Makes about 18.

Note: Overbeating causes muffin tops to have peaks. Mix only till just moistened!

The General Store of Fort Bragg

Herbed Garlic Bread

1/2 cup loosely packed flat-leaf parsley leaves, coarsely chopped

1/2 teaspoon fresh thyme, finely chopped

1 teaspoon fresh lemon juice

2 medium cloves garlic, minced

1/2 teaspoon Kosher salt

1/4 teaspoon freshly ground pepper

1/4 cup olive oil

1 12" long loaf sour dough French Bread

Heat oven to 350°.

Whisk together parsley, thyme, lemon juice, garlic, salt, pepper, and olive oil in a small bowl.

Using a bread knife slice the loaf into 12 half-inch slices, cutting three quarters of the way through the loaf so it stays intact. Brush the herb mixture generously between each slice.

Wrap the loaf loosely in foil. Heat until warm, about 10 minutes.

John Doughtery House of Mendocino

Scones Recipe

3 cups unbleached white flour
1 tablespoon baking powder
1/2 pound unsalted butter at room temperature
1/4 cup + 2 tablespoons white sugar
3 large farm eggs
1/3 cup buttermilk
1/2 cup golden raisins (sultanas)

Mix flour and baking powder in a bowl. In large "old stoneware bowl" beat until creamy. Add sugar and beat until pale and fluffy. Add eggs one at a time, beating after each. Add flour mixture; mix only until blended. Add butter-milk; mix only until blended. Sprinkle raisins over batter and fold in.

Using a large ice-cream scoop, place mounds of dough on an ungreased cookie sheet about 2 inches apart. Bake at 350° F for about 15 minutes. Cook on a wire rack.

Makes one dozen.

Well House West of Fort Bragg

Gayle Bowman's
Monka or Rice Waffles

1 cup milk
2 eggs, separated, whites stiffly beaten
1/2 teaspoon salt
1 cup flour
1 tablespoon sugar
2 teaspoons baking powder
4 tablespoons melted butter
1 cup cooked rice

Beat egg yolks; add sugar, milk, then flour sifted with the baking powder and salt. Add rice and melted butter. Beat egg whites stiff and add last.

Bake in Aebleskiver pan on top of stove. Place a dab of shortening in each hole-let melt and put spoon of batter in each hole. When done-with fork-flip ball over to fill out other side of ball. Serve with syrup, butter, jam, etc.

Although Monka are cooked in an Aebleskiver pan, this recipe makes wonderful rice waffles.

Little River Inn of Little River

Ole's Swedish Hotcakes

Mix the ingredients below together:

1 cup flour
1 teaspoon sugar
1/4 teaspoon salt
1 teaspoon baking powder

Combine with above mixed ingredients:

1 1/2 cup milk
1/2 cup half and half
3 eggs

Separate whites from yolks and beat whites until stiff. Beat yolks. Add yolks to batter. Then fold in whites of eggs. Add 3/4 cube of melted butter. This recipe serves four.

Honey Cake

Ingredients:

   2 1/2 cups honey

   1 cup water

   4 3/4 cups sifted flour

   2 tablespoons oil

   3 teaspoons cinnamon

   1/4 teaspoon cloves

   1 teaspoon salt

   2 1/4 teaspoons baking soda

   1 tablespoon lemon juice

Optional:

   Add a cup of candied ginger or citron cut into small chunks

Directions:

   Add the honey, water and oil into a pan. Heat the mixture on a low heat until it is thinned. Then add in the flour, cinnamon, cloves, baking soda, and salt. Mix thoroughly. Add the lemon juice last.

   Bake 1 hr. at 300° in a 10" x 13" pan.

   After removing the pan from the oven, allow it to cool and then remove it and place it on a cooling rack. Once it is cooled, it can be cut off the edges and then cut into 2 long loaves or 3 shorter loaves. Once the loaves are cut, wrap them tightly in aluminum foil and allow them to "age" for at least a week in a cool place like a pantry.

   Serve plain or lightly buttered.

   If it starts to get hard, it can be toasted. Honey is a natural preservative, so it keeps quite well! It's great with tea or coffee or just as a light snack.

   Enjoy! (brought by Cathy's Oma from Holland in 1923)

The Wool Loft Bed & Breakfast of Navarro Ridge

Refrigerator Coffee Cake

2 cups all purpose flour
2 teaspoons baking powder
3/4 tsp salt
1/2 cup sugar
6 tablespoons butter
1 egg beaten
1/2 cup milk

Grease and lightly four an 8 inch square pan. Blend flour, baking powder, salt, sugar, butter, egg, and milk. Pour batter into prepared pan.
Note: Double if you wish to, use a 9" x 13" pan.

Topping:
1-1/2 tablespoons butter, melted
1 tablespoon flour
4 tablespoons sugar
1 teaspoon cinnamon

In a small bowl combine ingredients. Spread over batter. Cover and refrigerate overnight. Bake at 350 degrees for 25 to 30 minutes.
Serves 6 to 8.

Spicy Pineapple Zucchini Bread

3 eggs

1 cup salad oil

2 cups sugar

2 teaspoons vanilla

2 cups (about 2 medium) zucchini, coarsely shredded, unpeeled

1 can (8 1/4 ounces) crushed pineapple, well drained

3 cups all-purpose flour, unsifted

2 teaspoons soda

1 teaspoon salt

1/2 teaspoon baking powder

1 1/2 teaspoons cinnamon, ground

3/4 teaspoon nutmeg, ground

1 cup walnuts, finely chopped

In a large bowl, beat eggs until frothy; add oil, sugar and vanilla; continue beating until mixture is thick and foamy. Stir in zucchini and pineapple (gently).

In a separate bowl, stir together flour, soda, salt, baking powder, cinnamon, nutmeg and walnuts. Stir gently into zucchini mixture until just blended. Spoon batter into 2 greased and flour-dusted loaf pans.

Bake at 350° for 1 hour or until a wooden toothpick inserted in the center comes out clean. Let cool in pans 10 minutes, then turn out onto racks to cool completely.

You can make apple or carrot bread by substituting shredded apple or carrot for zucchini.

Grey Whale Inn Bed & Breakfast of Fort Bragg

Cinnamon Nut Bread

6 cups sifted flour

1 tablespoon baking powder

1 1/2 teaspoon baking soda

1 1/2 teaspoon salt

3/4 cup unsalted butter or margarine

3 cups sugar

6 large eggs

3 cups buttermllk

1 tablespoon vanilla

2 cups walnuts, finely ground

6 tablespoons sugar

1 tablespoon cinnamon

Sift flour, baking powder, baking soda and salt. Cream butter and sugar. Add eggs, one at a time, beating well after each addition. Beat flour mix alternately with buttermilk into butter mixture, beginning and ending with flour mix. Stir in vanilla and walnuts. Pour half of batter into two greased and lightly floured 12-cup tube pans.

Combine remaining sugar and cinnamon. Sprinkle 3/4 of cinnamon-sugar mix over batter. Add remaining batter, sprinkle top with remaining cinnamon-sugar and swirl through batter with knife.

Bake at 350° until wooden pick comes out clean, about 50-60 minutes. Cool completely in pan on wire rack. Wrap and store in refrigerator.

Greenwood Lodge Cottages of Elk

Lemon-Nut Bread

1/2 cup butter

1 cup sugar

2 eggs, beaten

1 1/4 cup flour

1 teaspoon baking powder

dash of salt

1/2 cup mllk

grated peel of l lemon

juice from 1 lemon

1/2 cup walnuts, chopped

Cream butter and sugar. Add eggs. Alternately add milk and dry ingredients; then add lemon peel, lemon juice and nuts.

Bake in 9"x5"x3" greased pan for 1 hour or until wooden toothpick comes clean.

Topping:

  1/4 cup sugar

  juice of 1 lemon

Mix sugar and lemon juice together and pour over top of bread immediately after removing from oven.

Platt House of Fort Bragg

Easy French Toast

2 tablespoons light corn syrup

1/2 cup butter

1 cup light brown sugar

1 loaf sour dough whole grain un-sliced bread
    (I use Alvorado Street)

6 eggs

1 1/2 cups rich milk or half and half milk

1 teaspoon vanilla

1 teaspoon maple flavoring

In small saucepan, combine syrup, butter, and brown sugar. Simmer until syrupy. Pour over bottom of a well-greased 9x13 Pyrex container.

Slice bread, reasonably thick slices, and place over sugar mixture in dish.

Beat eggs, milk, vanilla, and maple flavoring. Pour over bread.

Cover and refrigerate overnight.

Bake at 350° uncovered for 45 minutes.

Serve hot. It might harden in the pan.

The Larkin Cottage of Mendocino

Custard French Toast

6 eggs + 3 egg yolks

1 1/2 cups sugar

1 tablespoon vanilla

4 cups milk

2 cups heavy cream

6 to 8 slices THICKLY cut bread (Texas toast)

1/2 cup sliced almonds

cinnamon

butter

powdered sugar

fruit syrup

Whisk together eggs, sugar and vanilla.
Add milk and cream.
Line a 9" x 13" buttered pan with the thick sliced bread.
Pour mixture over bread (bread will "float" to the surface).
Sprinkle with cinnamon and almonds.
Bake for 1 hour at 350°.
Let stand for 5—10 minutes before cutting.
Dust with powdered sugar and garnish with a squiggle of fruit syrup.

Blue Heron Inn & Moosse Cafe of Mendocino

Strawberry Rhubarb Breakfast Strudle

1 1/2 cups strawberries, diced
1 cup rhubarb, sliced thin
1 beaten egg
1/2 cup sugar
1 tablespoon corn starch
1/2 teaspoon cinnamon
1 sheet frozen puff pastry sheet 10" x 15"

Thaw pastry sheet. Brush lightly with beaten egg and dust with cinnamon.

Mix strawberries, rhubarb, corn starch and sugar (reserving 1 tablespoon sugar).

Spoon filling onto pastry, leaving 1" on each end. Roll up, egg washing pastry as you roll, folding ends.

Transfer to baking sheet with seam on bottom. Put 6 1" slits in top to allow steam to escape. Egg wash top and dust with remaining tablespoon of sugar.

Bake at 400° for 15-20 minutes, until pastry has risen and is golden brown.

North Coast Country Inn of Gualala

Quesadilla Breakfast Squares

2 cups shredded Cheddar cheese

2 cups shredded Jack Cheese

2 4-ounce cans green chilies, drained and diced

4 eggs, beaten to blend

2 cups milk

2 cups buttermilk biscuit mix

1/2 cup salsa

Toppings (optional):

> **sour cream**
>
> **Guacamole**
>
> **salsa**

Preheat oven to 425 degrees

Spray 9" x 13" baking dish with vegetable spray.

Sprinkle cheses in bottom of dish. Mix together.

Combine milk, baking mix and eggs in a large bowl and beat until smooth. Carefully pour over chilies. Top with 1/2 cup salsa.

Bake until puffed and golden for 25-30 minutes. Cool 10 minutes before serving.

Cut into squares and serve. Offer toppings as desired.

Serves 8-10.

The Weller House Inn of Fort Bragg

Open-face Soufflé Breakfast Sandwich

Per person:

> **1/2 sandwich size English muffin- toasted**
> **1 slice of honey-cured ham- thin**
> **1/2 cup mozzarella cheese**
> **1 egg- separated**
> **salt and pepper**

Place the toasted English muffin on a baking pan and lightly coat with butter. Place one ham slice on top. Set aside.

Whip the egg white until very firm. Gently add the yolk and cheese to the whipped white. Add a pinch of salt and fine ground black pepper. Place the egg mix on top of the ham slice.

Place in oven at 350° for 15-20 minutes until golden brown.

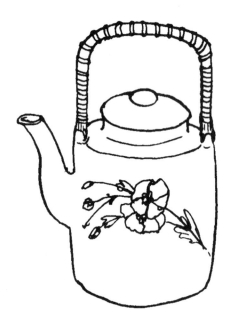

The Inn at Schoolhouse Creek of Little River

Basket Breakfast Pudding

2-1/2 cups left-over fresh fruit salad or fruit such as sliced peeled apples or pears; cranberries, strawberries or raspberries; or frozen un-sweetened blackberries, blue berries, strawberries, pitted tart red cherries, peach slices or sliced rhubarb; do not use citrus fruit.

3/4 cup sugar
1/4 cup margarine
1 cup all-purpose flour
1 teaspoon baking powder
1/2 teaspoon nutmeg
1/2 teaspoon salt
3/4 cup milk
Cinnamon Sugar

Thaw fruit if frozen. Spread fruit in square (9" x 9" x 2") baking dish.

In medium mixing bowl, beat the 3/4 cup sugar and margarine with electric mixer on medium speed until combined.

In a small bowl, stir together flour, baking powder, nutmeg, and salt. Beat into creamed mixture until combined (mixture will be crumbly.). Beat in milk until mixture is smooth.

Spread over fruit. Sprinkle with cinnamon sugar.

Bake pudding in a 350° oven for 40—50 minutes or until toothpick in-serted near center comes out clean.

Serve with fresh whipped cream.

Makes 6 to 8 servings.

Cleone Gardens Inn of Cleone

Garden Delight Breakfast Entree

1 canned corn beef (1202)

2 cups cheese (1/2 sharp & 1/2 mild)

1 cup pancake mix

2 cups milk

1 cup sliced mushrooms

1 tomato, chopped

1 cup red onion, diced

parsley

4 eggs (large)

1/4 teaspoon pepper

sour cream

Heat oven to 400°.

Spray vegetable spray on 9" x 13 1/2" baking dish. Spread onions, 1/2 cheese and corn beef on bottom of dish.

Hand mix (or blender 15 seconds) milk, egg, pancake mix pepper. Pour into dish, top with mushrooms and remaining cheese.

Bake for 40 minutes until center is firm. Cool. Cut into squares.

Top with dap of sour cream, tomato piece and parseley sprig for colorful presentation.

Serve with croisants and hot beverage. Can add salsa for added spice.

Makes 8-12 servings.

Soups
&
Salads

David's Delicatessen of Fort Bragg

Minestrone Soup

1/2 pound margarine
6 large carrots, cut bite size
3 large onions, cut bite size
6 cups celery, cut bite size
1 tablespoon garlic powder
crackers, any kind, crushed
1 can whole peeled tomatoes
1 can crushed tomatoes
1 head cabbage, cut bite size
4 sliced zuchinni, cut bite size
1 bunch bok choy, cut bite size
beef stock

Melt margarine in large pot and add carrots, onions, and celery. Sprinkle with garlic powder and cook over low heat until vegetables are medium tender. Add crackers, cans of tomatoes, and simmer for 1/2 hour. Add cabbage, zuchinni, bok choy, and beef stock.

Cook 3 to 4 hours.

Cultured Affair Cafe of Mendocino

Chicken Noodle Soup

1 pound skinless, boneless, chicken breast, diced
1 bottle beer (12 ounce)
1/2 green cabbage, chopped
1/4 cup dry onion
1 1/2 teaspoon minced garlic
1 carrot, chopped
1/4 teaspoon thyme
1 quart chicken broth (dilute with water if necessary)
3 ounces wide egg noodles

Combine all ingredients except noodles. Bring to boil and simmer 1 hour or until chicken is cooked. Add noodles and simmer 15 minutes. Season to taste with salt and pepper.

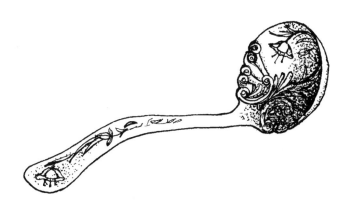

Soups & Salads

Headlands Coffee House of Fort Bragg

Darlene's Cream of Tomato Soup

2 28 ounce cans diced tomatoes

equal amount water

3 onions

4 cloves garlic

3 teaspoons sugar (or to taste)

3/4 teaspoon paprika

1 teaspoon basil

2 cups tomato juice

3 veggie boullion cubes

salt to taste

2 cups half & half or cream

Blend together tomatoes, water, onions, garlic, seasonings and juice until mixture is pureed. Cook stirring until mixture comes to a boil, simmer 20 minutes.

Stir in half & half or cream.

St. Orres of Gualala

Chilled Cantelope Soup

10 cantelope, peeled and seeded

1 cup apple juice

1 quart heavy cream

4 tablespoons brandy or casis

Blend cantelope and apple juice together. Strain into a container. Add heavy cream and brandy or casis.

Chill before serving.

Fetzer Vineyards Tasting Room of Mendocino

Cream of Broccoli Soup

4 cups chopped, fresh broccoli
   or 2 10-ounce packages frozen broccoli (thawed)
1/2 cup chopped onion
3 cups chicken stock
1/2 teaspoon thyme leaves
1/8 teaspoon garlic powder
1/4 cup Fetzer Valley Oaks Fume´
1/4 cup butter
1/4 cup unsifted flour
1/8 teaspoon pepper
1 pint light cream or milk

In a large saucepan, combine the broccoli, onion, chicken stock, thyme, garlic powder. Bring to a boil, reduce heat, cover, and simmer for 15 minutes, or until broccoli is tender.

Using 1/3 of the mixture at a time, blend until smooth in a blender or food processor. Add 1/4 cup Fetzer Valley Oaks Fume´ and return the now smooth mixture to the saucepan. Set aside.

Melt the butter in a medium saucepan over low heat. When melted, stir in the flour and pepper until smooth. Stir in cream. Cook and stir the mixture until thickened, then add it to the broccoli mixture. Heat the combined mixture together until hot; do not boil.

Serve hot or cold. Makes 1 1/2 quarts.

Serve this full-flavored soup with Fetzer Valley Oaks Fume´ as an accompaniment.

Chef for Hire of Mendocino

Chef Judith Henderson's
Rich Roasted Vegetable Soup

Set aside 6 cups rich vegetable stock or canned vegetable bouillion. Cut vegetables in 1" cubes, one cup each vegetable, and place in a large mixing bowl:

leeks
potato
carrot
turnip
celery
yellow onion
pear
apple

Toss cubed vegetables in 1/2 cup extra virgin olive oil, 4 cloves cracked garlic, and 1 teaspoon each:

kosher salt
white pepper
chopped fresh thyme
rosemary
1 crumpled Bay laurel leaf

Preheat oven to 350°. On a slightly oiled cookie sheet, place cut vegetables and roast for 45 minutes.

Remove roasted vegetables from oven. Divide half the vegetables and puree in a blender, using some of the vegetable stock to help liquify, to a thick but smooth consistancy.

In a 3 quart sauce pan, add pureed mixture to the rest of the roasted whole cubes of vegetables and the entire vegetable stock. Over medium heat, simmer gently and season to taste.

Offer a loaf of rustic whole wheat bread and butter, a tender assorted leaf salad with sliced blood oranges, yellow pear tomatoes, red onion slices and kiwi. Pass a bowl of freshly grated Asiago or Romano cheese to top the salad and a honey-soy Balsamic dressing.

Serves six.

Pot Gourmet of Mendocino

Curry Apple Salad

2 tablespoons mayonnaise
1 tablespoon peanut butter
3 tablespoons sugar
3 tablespoons vinegar (wine/raspberry, fruit flavor)
1/4 to 1/2 teaspoon cinnamon
1/8 teaspoon nutmeg
1/8 teaspoon curry
2/3 cup celery, finely chopped
1 large apple, unpeeled, cut in bite-size pieces
1/4 cup walnuts, chopped

Combine mayonnaise, peanut butter, sugar, vinegar, cinnamon, nutmeg, and curry. Blend well.
Add apple, celery, and walnuts. Toss well.
Serve on bed of lettuce. Garnish with chopped nuts.
Serves four to six.

Fuller's Fine Herbs of Mendocino

Mellissa's Buttermilk Salad Dressing

1 cup mayonaise
1 1/4 cup buttermilk
1 clove garlic, minced
1 1/2 teaspoon Fuller's Fine Herbs Dill Blend'*
      or 1 1/2 teaspoon dill
Fresh ground pepper—to taste

In a medium-size bowl combine the mayonaise and buttermilk until smooth. Add the Dill Blend, garlic and black pepper and mix well. Refrigerate at least one hour before serving.
This dressing also makes a delicious dip for fresh vegetables.
*Available on the Mendocino Coast or by mail.

Good Thyme Herb Blends of Mendocino

Debra Dawson's
Pesto Dressing for Pasta Salad

1/4 cup Dijon-style mustard, with or without mustard seeds

1/4 cup homemade or commercial pesto

1 tablespoon tamari or to taste

1/4 teaspoon pepper or to taste

dash Worcestershire sauce

1 cup mayonnaise

1 cup red wine vinegar

      —may be 1/2 cup Balsamic if desired

1 cup blended vegetable oil

      AND

1 cup cold-pressed olive oil

      OR

2 cups olive oil, if you wish

In the order given, combine all the ingredients in the Cuisinart with the steel blade, or by hand with a whisk.

To stay creamy and emulsified you must add the oil to the other well-combined ingredients. Use what you need and refrigerate the rest. This makes 1 quart or so and will dress over 4 pounds of pasta.

Good Thyme Herb Blends of Mendocino

Debra Dawson's
Quick Homemade Pesto for Salads & Pasta

1 generous bunch fresh basil, washed and patted dry in towel

6-10 large cloves garlic, peeled,
    depending on how much you like garlic

2 cups walnuts—pinenuts, of course, if you wish to pay that much,
    but walnuts do just fine

1 cup olive oil or thereabouts

1 tablespoon tamari or to taste

1/2 cup grated Parmesan, more on the table

In Cuisinart bowl, process garlic until finely chopped. Add walnuts and basil, also process until finely chopped. Add tamari, then olive oil gradually as you process to a fine paste. More oil will make it more liquid.

For salad dressings I use without Parmesan.

Keep refrigerated in a glass jar and use to add to sauces, salad dressings or to toss with pasta, using added Parmesan or Romano and more olive oil to taste.

Poultry
&
Meats

The Courtyard of Mendocino

Feta Stuffed Chicken with Almonds

2 whole chicken breasts with bone, split in half

8 ounces plain or seasoned Feta cheese

2 teaspoons dried oregano

1 tablespon butter, room temperature

2 teaspoons grated lemon zest

1/4 cup lemon juice

salt and freshly ground pepper

approximately 1/2 cup spinach

paprika

slivered almonds

Preheat oven to 425°.

Mix cheese, oregano, butter, lemon juice, lemon zest, salt, and ground pepper in small bowl.

Lift the chicken skin from the flesh without detaching it completely. Stuff cheese mixture under skin. Use as much as possible. Stuff spinach leaven on top of cheese mixture. If you have any cheese remaining, spread on top of chicken. Place in baking pan and sprinkle with paprika.

Bake for 30 minutes. Raise heat to 450° and bake 15 minutes.

Remove chicken from oven and sprinkle with slivered almonds. Serve immediately.

Serves four.

Fetzer Vineyards Tasting Room of Mendocino

Kathleen Fetzer's
Simply Elegant Tarragon Chicken

1 2 to 2 1/2 pound chicken, quartered
2-3 tablespoons butter
1/2 small onion, chopped fine
    (to give 3-4 tablespoons)
1 teaspoon dried tarragon
1/2 cup dry white wine
    (Fetzer Premium White)
1/2 cup water
salt and pepper

Melt the butter in a skillet large enough to hold all the chicken. Sprinkle the pieces of chicken with salt and pepper and add them (skin side down) to the skillet. Cook until the skin side is golden brown (8-10 minutes), then turn the pieces over and cook for another 4-5 minutes. Remove the chicken and set it aside.

Add the onions to the skillet and cook until just soft. Add the dried tarragon and the wine and keep cooking and stirring until you have a nice saucy mixture, then add the water. Put the chicken back in the skillet, with the golden side up, and cook covered for 10-15 minutes. Cook uncovered for 5-10 minutes more, basting the chicken with the sauce, until the chicken is tender. Serve this with rice and a green vegetable.

Accompanying wine: Fetzer Chenin Blanc

"With all the entertaining we do, I need to have some recipes at hand that can produce an elegant entree in a hurry. I have written this recipe to use a single chicken, quartered, to serve four. It can just as easily be adapted to a dozen chicken breasts, or several dozen chicken thighs—so long as you have pans big enough, increase the other ingredients, and watch the cooking time."

Greenwood Pier Cafe of Elk

Chicken Breasts in Sorrel Cream Sauce

3 chicken breasts, boned & skinned, halved

2 cups chicken stock

1 1/4 cup Fume Blanc

1/4 pound mushrooms

1 bunch fresh sorrel

2 cubes butter

1/2 cup heavy cream

1/2 cup flour

18 sheets phylo dough, 13" x 8 1/2"

Preparation:

Skin and bone the chicken breasts and halve. Melt 1 teapoon butter in heavy skillet, then add chicken stock, Fume Blanc, and chicken breasts. Poach over low heat for 12-15 minutes. Remove breasts & set aside; reserve stock for sauce.

Sauté mushrooms (slice if large) in butter and set aside; chop sorrel and sauté briefly until wilted, then transfer to blender and puree (or chop finely); set aside.

Make a paste by mixing 1/2 cup flour and 1/2 cup butter (1 cube) with a fork. Add to reserved stock and simmer over low heat stirring constantly until thickened; add 1/2 cup heavy cream and stir to blend; add final 1/4 cup McDowell Fume Blanc to give final flavor boost and simmer for 2 minutes before adding pureed sorrel and mushrooms. Adjust seasoning and remove from heat.

Assembly:

Melt final cube of butter; separate phylo dough and brush three sheets with butter and restack one on top of another. Place one of the chicken breasts near corner, spoon sauce on breast and roll up, giving a final brush to outer surface of dough. Repeat for all breasts before placing in a baking dish.

Bake:

Bake in preheated oven at 400° for approximately 15 minutes or until golden brown.

Presentation:

Spoon any remaining sauce on plate, place puffed chicken breast in center and garnish with fresh owers or parsley.

Serves 6 persons.

Fuller's Fine Herbs of Mendocino

Arlene & Michael Fuller's
Herb & Cheese Baked Chicken

1 whole medium-sized chicken

12 ounces cream cheese

1/2 cup Gruyere or Asiago cheese, grated

1 small zucchini, grated

1 clove garlic, crushed

1 tablespoon butter

2 teaspoons Fuller's Beaujolais Blend*

1/8 teaspoon white pepper

1/8 teaspoon salt

Pre-heat oven to 325°.

Melt butter in small skillet and sauté the zucchini until tender. Transfer to a strainer and allow the juice from the zucchini to drain.

Wash the chicken and pat it dry with towels.

In a large bowl blend together the cream cheese, grated cheese, zucchini, garlic, Fuller's Beaujolais Blend, pepper, and salt. Holding the chicken firmly, slip your fingers between the skin and the meat (at the leg end) and gently loosen the skin along the breast, legs, and back, to make a pocket for the cheese mixture. Holding the pocket between skin and flesh open, stuff small scoops of the cheese mixture under the skin of the chicken until chicken is plump-looking all over.

Place chicken in a baking dish and bake approximately 1 hour and 10 minutes (a bit longer for a larger bird).

The Melting Pot of Mendocino

Skip's Chicken Mendocino

4 to 6 half chicken breasts, preferably boned
Mendocino Mustard
　　　—a product locally produced and available at markets and
specialty stores on the Mendocino Coast—a good, hot sweet mustard
blend may be substituted
　　1 cup seasoned bread crumbs
　　1/2 cup Parmesan cheese
　　1 cup chicken broth or bouillion (stock)
　　heavy cream

Remove all skin from boned chicken breasts and form into a compact ball. Coat completely all sides of breasts with Mendocino Mustard. Combine bread crumbs with Parmesan cheese, mixing well. Completely cover breasts with crumb mixture.

Place in an ungreased baking dish. Bake in a pre-heated oven at 350° for 30 minutes. Prepare chicken stock and add to baking dish (the stock must be hot to avoid shock breakage of baking dish). Bake for additional 30 minutes, basting breasts about every 10 minutes.

Lightly brown breasts under the broiler for a few seconds; then remove cooked breasts from pan to serving plate.

Prepare a gravy or sauce from the remaining liquid; add more Mendocino Mustard to taste. Add heavy cream as necessary.

Drizzle sauce over breasts and serve with steamed snow peas with water chestnuts.

*Available on the Mendocino Coast or by mail.

Bay View Cafe of Mendocino

Chicken Vera Cruz

2 tablespoons olive or vegetable oil

6 chicken thighs, skin removed

1 large onion, chopped

1 green bell pepper, seeded, chopped

1/2 pound mushrooms, each cut in half

1-16 ounce can diced tomatoes

1-8 ounce can tomato sauce

1-4 ounce can diced Ortega chilis

1 1/2 tablespoons chili powder

2 teaspoons cumin powder

1 teaspoon dried oregano leaves

salt and pepper

Sauté chicken thighs in oil until lightly browned. Add onion, green pepper, mushrooms, and sauté for 5 minutes over medium heat. Add remaining ingredients excluding salt and pepper. Add just enough water to cover chicken. Simmer on low for 45 minutes to 1 hour, until chicken is tender, adding more water if necessary. Season with salt and pepper to taste. Remove chicken bones if you wish.

Serve with tortillas, rice or polenta.

Serves 4 to 6.

Pacific Star Winery of Fort Bragg

Chateaubriand with Charbono Mushroom Sauce and Baked Onion

large Chateaubriand (London broil) 1 1/2 to 2" thick, cut
    (about 2 lb.)
2 cups Charbono (A Pacific Star wine, any dry red wine is OK)
3 cups sliced, fresh mushrooms (We use porcini if possible)
    or 3 ounces dried
4 cloves garlic
2 sprigs rosemary
2 sprigs oregano
small bunch basil
4 large yellow onions
olive oil

Marinate the beef in wine, garlic, rosemary, oregano and basil. Ideally for 6-8 hours (4 hours minimum).

Trim the ends of the onions and peal dry skins away. Place in a lightly oiled shallow casserole. Drizzle with olive oil. Sprinkle each with a few rosemary and oregano leaves. Bake uncovered at 350 degrees for about 45 minutes until onions are soft and glazed slightly.

Grill steak on mesquite or grape wood barbecue. We like this beef slightly pink inside, so about 7-8 minutes per side.

While the steak is grilling, pour the remaining marinade into a small skillet with the mushrooms. Sauté mushrooms in liquid about ten minutes until tender, not mushy. Remove mushrooms with a slotted spoon and reduce the liquid by 1/2. Return mushrooms to sauce.

Make a bed with 1/3-1/2 an onion, top with diagonally cut thin slices of beef. Top with sauce.

Serves 8-12

Moore Used Books of Mendocino

Blanche Grossnickle's Casserole

2 pounds ground beef

2 cloves garlic

2 teaspoons salt

1 teaspoon pepper

2 teaspoons sugar

3-#2 cans tomato sauce

1-8 ounce package cream cheese

2 cups sour cream

2 bunches green onions, chopped

2-3 cups cheddar cheese, grated

1 8-ounce package noodles, any size

Brown beef, add garlic, salt, pepper, sugar; mix well. Add tomato sauce, cover and simmer 15-20 minutes. Cook noodles and drain. Soften cream cheese and mix with sour cream and green onions. Place 1/3 of the noodles in large casserole and cover with layer of sour cream mixture. Top with meat sauce. Repeat layering until all ingredients are used up. Sprinkle with grated cheese and bake at 350° until hot and bubbly (approximately 45 minutes).

Freezes well. (If frozen, double baking time and top with cheese for last 15 minutes of baking).

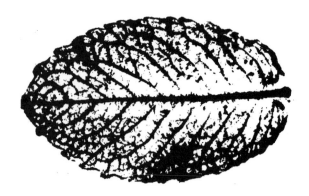

Heritage House of Little River

Black Bean Chili

2 cups bacon, small dice

1 onion, small dice

1 clove garlic, small dice

1 pound sirloin steak, cut into 1/4-inch strips

3 cups black beans

1 cup red wine

2 whole tomatoes, peeled

10 cups beefstock

3 bay leaves

1 tablespoon cumin

2 tablespoons chili powder

1/4 teaspoon cayenne pepper

1/4 cup fresh cilantro

creme fraiche

Sauté bacon crisp; then add onion and garlic; brown. Add sirloin, brown, then add rest of ingredients. Cook for 2 to 2 1/2 hours. While cooking you might have to adjust the liquid with more stock.

Serve with crème fraîche and chopped cilantro.

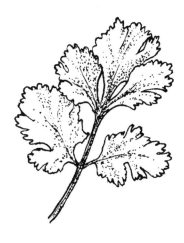

Café Vienna of Fort Bragg

Café Vienna Goulasch

2 pounds chuck meat, cut into 1" cubes

4 pounds red onions, diced

2 ounces Hungarian paprika

1 tablespoon Hungarian hot papriles

1 1/2 teaspoon salt

dash black pepper

sour cream

Variations:
> Add:
>> 1 clove garlic
>>
>> tomato paste for added color
>>
>> diced potato

Simmer meat for 2 to 3 hours with just enough water to cover meat. Cook diced onions slowly over low flame until soft, approximately 1 hour. Puree onions. Stir puree and spices into water and meat. Add more water if necessary. Cook for 1 more hour. Top with a dab of sour cream. Serve with dumplings, noodles, rice and/or bread.

Serves six.

Guten Apetit!

Drummond Farms of Mendocino

Caribbean Ginger Pear BBQ Ribs

1 medium onion, finely chopped

4-5 cloves garlic, minced

2 Serrano or Jalapeno chilies, seeded and minced

2 tablespoons oil

 cup dark beer

1/4 cup rice or white wine vinegar

3/4 cup Drummond Farms Ginger Pear Chutney

1—6 ounce can pineapple juice

1/2 cup brown sugar

1 tablespoon tomato paste

1/2 teaspoon cup cayenne pepper (optional)

1 large rack of ribs

Heat the oil in a sauce pan until hot, but not smoking. Sauté the onion, garlic and chilies over high heat until the onion turns translucent. Add the beer and vinegar. Continue cooking over high heat until the volume has been reduced by half. Add Drummond Farms Ginger Pear Chutney, pineapple juice, brown sugar, tomato paste and cayenne pepper.

When the sauce returns to a boil, reduce heat to medium. Using a potato masher, mash the sauce until the pears and onions have been blended in and the sauce is no longer chunky. Continue to simmer, stirring frequently for 15-20 minutes. Remove 3/4 cup of the sauce for the marinade. Reduce heat to low. Simmer remaining sauce, uncovered, for 10-15 minutes, until the sauce has reduced to the desired thickness. Remove from heat and set aside until ready to serve.

Place the rack of ribs on a dish or platter. Cover with the 3/4 cup of sauce removed for the marinade. Marinate for an hour at room temperature. Grill over a low charcoal fire, turning as needed. Serve the remaining thickened sauce on the side.

This is our favorite barbecue sauce for ribs. We also use it for pork loin and chops, chicken, shrimp, and sausage.

Mendocino Gift Company of Mendocino

Porcupine Balls

1 1/2 pounds hamburger or ground turkey
1 egg
salt and pepper to taste
1 1/2-2 cups instant rice
2 cans tomato soup or mushroom soup (milk-2 soup cans)
1 tablespoon oil

Mix together all ingredients except soup/milk and oil. Form large meat balls. Place oil in bottom of dutch oven. Put in meat balls and bake uncovered in 425° oven for 15 minutes or until browned slightly. Add soup and put milk into soup cans to rinse remainder of soup and pour over meat balls and soup. Cover and bake for 25 minutes at 375°.

Serve with salad.

Wine World at Anchor Bay Village Market
Anchor Bay

Italian Sausage Stew

1 pound Italian sauage, mild or hot
6 red potatoes, chopped
1 small head green cabbage, quartered
1 cup dry white wine

Sauté sausage until well done. Place chopped potatoes on top of sausage. Place cabbage on top of potatoes. Pour one cup white wine over cabbage.

Simmer, covered, for 30 minutes over medium heat on top of stove. Done when potatoes pierce easily with a fork.

Serve with salad, garlic bread, and your favorite bottle of white or red wine!

The Blue Victorian Inn & Antique Shop of Westport

Crying Lamb

6-9 pound leg of lamb
1/4 cup olive oil
6 cloves garlic, 2 slivered, 4 chopped
1 tablespoon rosemary, chopped
2 tablespoons thyme, chopped
salt and pepper to taste
12 potatoes, peeled and thinly sliced
3 tablespoons butter, cubed

Rub leg of lamb with oil. Make gashes in the lamb and poke the garlic slivers in. Dust leg with chopped herbs and sprinkle with salt and pepper.

Layer potatoes in roasting pan that is bigger than leg. Sprinkle potatoes with salt, pepper, chopped garlic and cubed butter. Set potatoes dish on second oven rack.

Place lamb on first rack so drippings fall onto potatoes. This is the lamb crying.

Roast for 1 1/2 hours at 425° F. Stir potatoes often and reduce heat if potatoes brown too quickly. Carve meat and serve on potatoes.

St. Orres of Gualala

Venison aux Cerises

Loin of venison sauteed and served with a demi-glaze, shallots and dark sweet cherries.

1-3-pound loin of venison

Marinade:

2 medium carrots, peeled and cut into 3-inch lengths
2 medium celery stalks, cut into 3-inch lengths
4 medium onions, quartered
1/2 fifth of dry vermouth
10 Juniper berries
1 head of garlic, halved
4 tablespoons fresh thyme, chopped
10 sprigs parsley
20 black peppercorns
2 bay leaves

Mix all ingredients together in a large bowl. Marinate loin in this mixture for 24 hours, turning once. Strain marinade; set aside liquid.

Portion venison into 8 servings. Lightly salt and pepper venison, brown in peanut oil on all sides; approximately 2 minutes per side. Remove venison to warm platter.

Cherry sauce:

4 tablespoons chopped shallots
16 ounces of reserved marinade liquid
16 ounces demi-glaze (beef stock reduced half)
16 1/2 ounce can of dark sweet pitted cherries
1/2 cup cherry liquid
2 tablespoons sweet butter

Reduce shallots, demi-glaze and cherry liquid by half. Add drained cherries. Remove from heat, swirl in butter. Salt & pepper to taste. Pour over venison and serve.

Serves eight.

Fish
&
Seafood

Harbor House of Elk

Ling Cod Kiev

6 medium to thick Ling [Pacfic] cod filets
1 cube sweet butter, softened
1/4 cup finely chopped chives
1/4 cup minced parsley
2 tablespoons dill weed
1 tablespoon salt
1 cup cornstarch
4 eggs, beaten until just foamy
1/2 cup sesame seeds
1 cup bread or cracker crumbs
6 tablespoons butter
6 tablespoons oil

Dry filets. Make a horizontal pocket in each piece. Cream butter and herbs well. Spread about 2 teaspoons or more of butter mixture into the pocket. Press opening shut. Roll filet in cornstarch, then egg, then sesame seeds mixed with the crumbs. Lay in pan lined with paper towels and refrigerate until time to cook.

Preheat a skillet with olive oil and butter until sizzling. Cook filets about 4 minutes per side, depending on thickness.

Serves six.

Mendosa's of Mendocino

Larry De Quincy's
Chinese or Vietnamese Steamed Fish

1 whole cabezone (or ling cod)
green onions, sliced
ginger, sliced
canola oil
soy sauce

Cut the head off. Cut the fins off. Cut the tail off. Clean it. Leave the skin on.

Make a bed of sliced green onions, cut up the long way, and very thinly sliced ginger.

Put a lot of onions and ginger inside the cavity and on top.

Steam until the fish flakes.

Put the canola oil and soy sauce into a frying pan until it begins to bubble.

Pour over fish and serve, together with rice.

One of the most famous dishes in Asia.

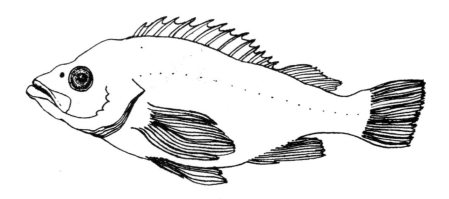

Fish & Seafood

Mendosa's of Mendocino

Chuck Moffett's
Chioppino

1 cup olive oil
1 can flat anchovies, chopped
2 onions, chopped
1 cup celery, chopped
2 cloves garlic, chopped
1/2 cup parsley, chopped
1 large can (#2 1/2) whole tomatoes
1 6 ounce can tomato paste + 1 can water
1 8 ounce can tomato sauce
optional herbs—bay, basil—to taste
salt & pepper to taste
1 quart wine (red or white or both)
3 crabs, cleaned (in shell), cracked if desired
3 pounds small clams
2 pounds raw prawns

Heat olive oil in large pot.

Sauté anchovies, onions, celery, garlic, and parsley for 15 seconds and add to the large pot.

Add tomatoes, tomato paste and water, tomato sauce, herbs, salt and pepper to the large pot.

Simmer about 1/2 hour.

(At this point, may be refrigerated or frozen for later use.)

Add wine.

Simmer on low for 2-4 hours.

About 20 minutes before serving, add crabs, clams and prawns.

Return to stove and simmer about 10-20 minutes.

Serve in bowls, with French bread.

(For larger quantities, increase all ingredients except olive oil and anchovies.)

Fish & Seafood

Stevenswood Lodge of Little River

Chef Marc Dym's
Bouillabaisse

1/2 cup olive oil
4 cloves peeled garlic, chopped
1 each large carrot, julienne
1 each medium onion, julienne
1 each leek, julienne
1 each fennel bulb, julienne
2 each celery stalks, julienne
4 each Roma tomatoes, diced
1 teaspoon dry basil
1 teaspoon dry oregano
1 teaspoon dry thyme leaves
1 each bay leaf
1 teaspoon dry marjoram
1/2 teaspoon rosemary
2 teaspoons salt
1/2 teaspoon white pepper
1 teaspoon saffron
1 cup dry Vermouth
1 cup white wine
1/4 cup Pernod
4 cups clam juice
4 cups tomato juice
8 each large shrimp
4 each lobster tails, split
8 each large scallops
8 each 2 ounce Monkfish pieces
16 each Manilla clams
16 each mussels

In a large soup pot add olive oil and sauté chopped garlic. Add vegetables and cook until tender. Add dried herbs. Deglaze with wine and pernod. Add clam and tomato juice. Bring to a simmer. Lower heat and add seafood. Cook until clams and mussels open and fish is cooked.

Serves four.

Albion River Inn of Albion

Baked Marinated Albacore

albacore
red wine
tamari
garlic & shallots
bay leaf
black pepper corns, crushed
brown sugar
parsley

Make marinade to taste, slightly sweet, lots of garlic. Mix tamari and red wine, with the red wine being the dominate one.

Cut albacore into small 4-ounce medallions and put in marinade overnight.

Bake in small amount of marinade until flesh feels firm. Then garnish with leftover marinade and parsley.

Harvest Market of Fort Bragg

Carol Price's Prize-Winning
Marinated BBQ Salmon—North Coast Style

1 jar roasted garlic non-oil marinade
1/2 cup fresh parsely, chopped
1/2 cup Worcestershire Sauce
1/2 cup soy sauce
1 cup white wine
the juice of one lemon
a pinch of oregano
a dash of hot pepper sauce

Whisk together all ingredients. Pour 1/2 of mixture into marinade dish and place salmon in pan, skin side up. Pour remaining mixture over salmon and let sit for at least two hours, or even overnight.

Place salmon skin side down on hot grill. Cook five minutes or until salmon separates from skin. Turn salmon over with large spatula, leaving skin on grill. Place salmon back on skin. baste with marinade from pan often until done (about five more minutes).

Transfer to hot serving platter. Serve with Spinach Salad and Garlic Bread and dream sweet dreams of the blue Pacific!

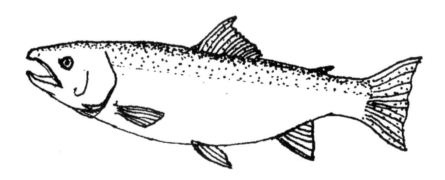

Fish & Seafood

Elk Cove Inn of Elk

Chef Trudy Lenzi-Tocco's
Salmon Burger

1 1/2 pounds salmon filet
2 teaspoons salt
1 finely diced red bell pepper
2 eggs
1 bunch green onions
1/4 cup cream or half & half
1/4 teaspoon cayenne
1 cup bread crumbs

Hand chop salmon. Add rest of ingredients—adjust bread crumbs for right consistency.

Makes 6 servings.

Green Tartar Sauce:
1 large shallot
3 tablespoons parsley
3 tablespoons capers
2 tablespoons fresh dill
1/4 cup chopped cornichons
1 teaspoon lemon juice
3/4 cup mayonnaise
1/2 teaspoon Dijon
3 tablespoons fresh chives
1/2 teaspoon pepper

Combine all of the above in Cuisinart.

Greenwood Pier Inn of Elk

Smoked Salmon Quiche

Crust:

> **1 1/2 cups flour**
> **1 teaspoon salt**
> **1/2 cup shortening**
> **2 tablespoons water**

Mix ingredients together into a ball, chill for 30 minutes, then roll out and place in a greased pie plate.

Filling:

> **1/4 pound smoked salmon**
> **1/4 cup green onions, chopped**
> **1/4 cup parsley**
> **1/4 cup cream cheese**
> **3 eggs**
> **1/4 cup sour cream**
> **1/4 cup half & half**
> **1/4 cup hard cheese, grated**

Place parsley and green onions on unbaked pie crust. Then salmon and cream cheese are put evenly over the parsley and green onions.

Mix eggs and half & half, then pour over ingredients in pie plate.

Sprinkle grated cheese over it all.

Bake 45 minutes at 350°.

Fuller's Fine Herbs of Mendocino

Shrimp 'Para-Creole'

1 small onion, chopped fine

1/2 large red bell pepper, coarsely chopped

1 stalk celery, diced

1 tablespoon butter

1 tablespoon oil

1 1/2 teaspoon Fuller's Paravangna Blend*

1 teaspoon sugar

1 pound shrimp

1/4 cup dry sherry

1 large can tomatoes with juice (about 2 1/2 cups), coarsely cut up

salt to taste

about 4 cups steamed rice

Melt the butter and oil in a large pan or pot (preferably stainless steel). Saute the onion, pepper and celery until they are tender. Add the Fuller's Paravangna Blend and cook about 1 minute more. Add the chopped tomatoes with the juices and sugar and simmer gently 10-15 minutes.

Stir in the sherry and shrimp; simmer 5 minutes more. DO NOT BOIL or the shrimp will become tough and dry.

Taste and season with salt if desired.

Serve over steamed rice; white rice is attractive and tasty with this particular dish.

A cold beer or a nice dry white wine is nice served with the creole.

*Available on the Mendocino Coast or by mail.

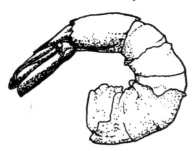

The Nye Ranch of Fort Bragg

Jay Gray's
Clam Pasta and French Bread

1 medium onion
5 cloves garlic
1/2 cube butter
1 cup white wine
2 8-ounce cans minced clams
1/2 teaspoon white pepper
1/2 teaspoon salt
1 tablespoon cornstarch
2 tablespoons oil
about 5 cloves garlic for bread

Sauté onions, garlic, salt and pepper in oil. Add minced clams, butter, wine and simmer, for an hour or so. Add more wine if necessary. Before serving mix your cornstarch in clam juice and add to your sauce to thicken. Serve over Ronzoni pasta #8.

To go with your pasta you want to have garlic bread. Cut a long loaf of French bread in half, length-wise. Broil in oven until brown. Take your peeled garlic cloves and rub into hot bread (it will just melt away!). Put your butter on and pop back into the oven for a few minutes. Cut up and serve all at once.

Have a nice green salad with this, also.

Elk Cove Inn of Elk

Chef Trudy Lenzi-Tocco's
Clam Chowder

10 ounce Hickory Smoked bacon, rendered/caramelized

 tablesoon fresh chopped thyme or 1/2 teaspoon dried thyme

4 medium sized yellow onions, diced

2 carrots, diced

1/4 teaspoon ground pepper

8 ribs celery, diced

1/2 teaspoon hot sauce

4 large russet potatoes, peeled, diced

1/2 teaspoon salt

1 cup dry white wine

1 tablespoon Worcestershire sauce

1 #3 can chopped ocean clams

1/2 cup flour

1 tablespoon minced garlic

3/4 cup heavy cream

Add onions and garlic to bacon, cook until clear. Add and sauté carrots, celery, thyme, salt, and pepper about 5 minutes.

Pour in wine, reduce until syrupy, add potatoes and sauté about 10 minutes.

Add drained clam juice, cook until potatoes and vegies are done.

Add flour, hot sauce and Worcestershire, cook until flour dissolved-add clams and cream (enough for desired consistency)—heat until hot.

Salt & pepper to taste.

Vegetables, Grains, Pastas & Casseroles

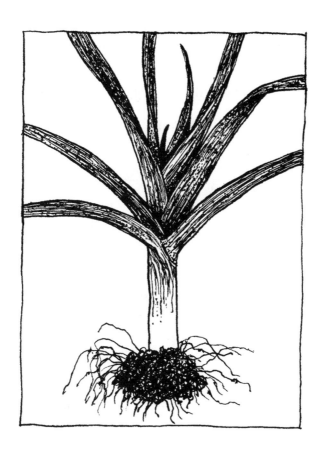

Judy Summers'
Curried Cauliflower

2 pounds cauliflower

1/2 cup vegetable oil

1/2 teaspoon black or brown mustard seed

1/2 teaspoon cumin seed

1 teaspoon ginger root, minced or finely chopped

1/2 cup onion, finely chopped

1 teaspoon salt

1/2 teaspoon turmeric

1 28 ounce can chopped tomatoes

1 fresh hot chili, seeded and finely chopped

1 tablespoon ground cumin

3 tablespoons fresh cilantro, finely chopped

Wash and trim cauliflower, divide into small flowerets, and dry thoroughly. Set aside.

In a heavy 4-5 quart casserole or large pot, heat the oil over moderate heat until a light haze forms above it. Stir in the mustard seeds, then immediately add the cumin seeds, ginger, and onions. Cook, stirring constantly for 1 minute—add the salt and turmeric, and continue cooking for 3-4 minutes.

Drop in the cauliflower and turn the flowerets about with a spoon until they are evenly coated with the onion mixture. Then stir in the tomatoes, chili, ground cumin, and 1 tablespoon of the fresh cilantro. Reduce the heat to low, cover and cook until the cauliflower is just tender. Stir frequently and check doneness so as not to overcook.

Transfer to serving dish or plate and garnish with the remaining cilantro. Serves four to six.

Caspar Institute of Caspar

Artichaux Casparienne

2 cans whole artichoke hearts

2 lemons

1 cup clean fresh mushrooms

1/4 cup oil

2 cloves garlic, diced fine

sprig fresh basil (or *lots* of dried)

1/2 cup strong bouillon or consomme

1/2 cup white wine

1 dozen cherry tomatoes, sliced

 teaspoon arrowroot

capers

Drain cans of whole Artichoke Hearts.

Juice lemons and remove seeds—keep pulp.

Slice the clean, fresh mushrooms.

Heat sauteuse (large, shallow saucepan) and add 1/4 cup oil. Immediately add diced garlic, basil and sliced mushrooms. Sautee´ until the mushrooms start to yield their liquor.

Add the lemon juice, bouillon or consomme and white wine—any nice wine will do—and reduce the flame to a gentle boil to cook the wine. As soon as the bitter taste of cooking wine has cooked away, remove a few tablespoons of juice and cool in a shallow bowl.

Correct the seasoning for the sauce and add the sliced tomatoes. Add arrowroot to the cooled sauce, mix well, then add to the main and stir it until it thickens. Immediately lower the heat to the barest simmer and add the artichokes. Set them open side up and spoon juice over them until they are thoroughly filled. Add capers. Cover and simmer for a few minutes until the artichokes are piping hot.

Serve over rice as a main course, or alone as a vegetable dish.

The Old Milano Hotel of Gualala

Chilled Asparagus with Lemon Cream

1 pound fresh asparagus [trim & butt ends, peel if large
 —2 to 3 bunches tied]
1/2 cup heavy cream
 large lemon [zest and juice]
salt

For asparagus, have a large pot of salted water at a rapid boil. Cook asparagus uncovered just until done. Watch carefully so they don't over-cook. When done, fish bundles out of water and immediately immerse in ice water. When cold, drain and refrigerate. Asparagus may be cooked no more than one day ahead.

For cream, whip cream until stiff. Salt to taste. Add lemon zest and juice. Put the cream in a bowl and arrange asparagus on a plate. Dip the asparagus in the cream.

Fetzer Vineyards Tasting Room of Mendocino

Kelly Trost's
Wild Mushroom & Pecan Tart

2 1/2 cups whole pecans

1/2 cup cracker crumbs

1/2 cup butter, melted

2 cups Cremini mushrooms

3 cups assorted wild mushrooms

1 cup scallions, finely chopped

1 cup parsley, finely coppped

3 cloves garlic, minced

2 tablespoons butter

1 cup Chardonnay

1 cup blue cheese, crumbled

1/2 cup Parmesan

3 tablespoons seasoned bread crumbs

In food processor, finely chop pecans. Blend pecans, cracker crumbs and butter and press into 9" pan. Bake at 350° until golden, about 15 minutes. Remove from oven and allow to cool.

Finely chop all mushrooms. Melt butter in large sauté pan and cool mushrooms, scallions, parsely and garlic until all liquid has evaporated. Add Chardonnay and cook again until liquid has evaporated.

Sprinkle blue cheese in bottom of tart shell. Spoon mushroom mixture on top and spread evenly. Top with Parmesan and bread crumbs. Bake at 350° just until Parmesan has melted and tart is warmed through.

Serve immediately.

Mendocino Mushrooms of Mendocino
"Highest Quality Wild Mushrooms"

Mushroom Burgers

1/2 ounce dry wild mushrooms

2 1/2 cups fresh mushrooms, chopped

1 cup plus 2 tablespoons bread crumbs

2/3 cup low fat cottage cheese

1/2 cup onions, chopped

2 large eggs, lightly beaten

2 1/4 ounces mozzerella cheese, shredded

2 ounces walnuts, chopped

1 teaspoon reduced sodium soy sauce

1 or 2 cloves garlic

black pepper to taste

Combine all ingredients, except oil. Shape into patties.

Preheat oven to 325°.

Fry patties in oil until nice and brown on both sides. Spraying the pan with Pam helps reduce amount of oil needed.

Bake 15 minutes in oven.

These freeze very well. They can be reheated in the microwave. They are really delicious!!

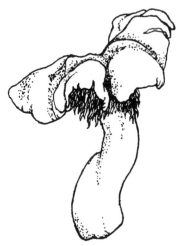

Little River Restaurant of Little River

Basil and Lemon Potato Gratin

2 pounds Yukon Gold potatoes, peeled and sliced thin
1 bunch fresh basil leaves, chopped
1/4 teaspoon freshly grated nutmeg
zest of 1 lemon, finely grated
salt and ground pepper to taste
1 cup half and half
butter

Heat oven to 400°.

Brush a 10" x 5" gratin dish with melted butter. Cover the bottom of the dish with an even layer of potatoes. Sprinkle one third of the basil, nutmeg and lemon zest on the potatoes. Salt and pepper, dot with butter. Add a second layer same as the first. Top with a third layer of potato slices and arrange neatly. Pour half and half over the potatoes and sprinkle with remaining basil, nutmeg, lemon zest, salt and pepper. Dot with butter.

Cover with foil; place on center rack of oven, and bake for 40 minutes. Remove foil and continue to bake for 10 to 20 more minutes until golden brown and tender when pierced with a sharp fork.

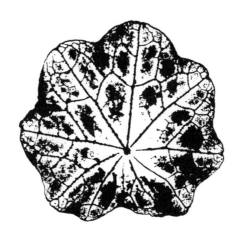

Vegetables, Grains, Pastas & Casseroles

Mendocino Sea Vegetable Company of Navarro

Eleanor Lewallen's
Wakame, Cabbage & Bean Thread

1 cabbage
1 cup boiled wakame
2 tablespoons safflower oil
2 carrots, grated
2 teaspoons ginger, crushed
4 cloves garlic, crushed
2 to 3 tablespoons honey
2 tablespoons soy sauce
1/2 teaspoons sesame oil
2 ounces dried bean thread

Cut the boiled wakame into 1-inch by 1/4-inch strips. Soak the bean threads in 3 cups of water until soft. Shred the cabbage.

Sauteé ginger and garlic in a wok until it is just golden. Add wakame, cabbage, carrots and bean threads; then add soy sauce and honey, adjusting flavors to taste. Sauteé until done (5 to 8 minutes). Add more water if necessary to keep this dish moist during cooking.

This dish may be served hot over rice or cold as a salad.

Sai Poma Ranch of Comptche

Vegetable Garlic Casserole

3 zucchini, sliced in 1/4-inch slices
3 medium potatoes
peeled and sliced in 1/4-inch slices
2 bell peppers, sliced
1 medium-sized eggplant, peeled and sliced
1/4 cup oil
3 large elephant garlic, sliced very thin
1 large onion, sliced
4 large tomatoes or 1 pound can tomatoes
1/4 teaspoon salt
1/8 teaspoon pepper
1/2 teaspoon oregano
4 tablespoons grated cheese

Layer vegetables alternately in a casserole with 2 tablespoons grated cheese sprinkled between each layer.

For the sauce: Sauté the onion and garlic in oil until color changes, add the tomato, herbs, and seasoning and simmer until done.

Pour over the layered vegetables, cover top with balance of cheese, and bake covered for 1 hour at 350°; then uncover and bake another hour.

Serves four or five.

Cafe Prima of Fort Bragg

Ivory Coast Pasta Sauce

1 cup tomato puree

1/4 cup chopped shalots

1/2 cup chopped onions

1/2 tablespoon chopped garlic

1 cup coconut milk

1/2 half cup chopped tomatoes (peeled are preferred)

1 pinch cardamon seed

1/2 teaspoon tumaric powder

1/4 cup dried raisins

1/2 teaspoon garam marsala (Indian spice mixture)

1/2 cumin powder

1 pinch oregano

1 anise seed

1/2 teaspoon parsley

Put tomato puree in pan, turn on low.

Put coconut milk, onions, shalots and cardamon seeds into blender. Rough blend. Put this blend, and all other ingredients—except chopped tomatoes—into pan with tomato puree. Keep heat on low. Add necessary water for desired consistency. Cook for 20 to 25 minutes.

While cooking, cook pasta. Add tomatoes to pan, salt to taste.

After all is cooked, toss sauce and pasta together and serve, with cheese (like Parmesan) if desired.

Serves 4.

Vegetables, Grains, Pastas & Casseroles

Old Sewart House Inn of Fort Bragg

Frencazina

Grandmother's recipe from Lucca, Italy

4 eggs

2 cups homemade tomato-based spaghetti sauce

4 slices toast

Parmesan cheese (to sprinkle)

In a frying pan, slowly heat the spaghetti sauce. Add the eggs to the top of the sauce. Cook slowly to preference of sunny-side up or over-easy. Put one egg and some sauce on each of the slices of toast. Sprinkle with cheese. Serve.

Mendocino Village Inn of Mendocino

Maria's Chiliquilles

10-12 tortillas, cut into 1/2x2-inch strips

1 large onion, chopped

1 clove garlic, minced

4 tablespoons butter

1 dozen eggs, beaten

salt, pepper and cumin to taste

1 can green chilies, chopped

1/2 cup sharp cheese, grated

1 tomato, peeled & chopped

Sauteé tortilla strips, chopped onion and garlic in butter until soft. Beat eggs. Add milk, salt, pepper and cumin. Pour eggs over tortilla mixture. Cook, stirring until soft and scrambled. Add green chilies, cheese and tomato. Stir until cheese melts.

Garnish with cilantro.

The Melting Pot of Mendocino

Chili Relleno Casserole

1 pound cheddar cheese, grated
1/2 pound Monterey jack cheese, grated
2 4-ounce cans whole green chiles
4 eggs
2 tablespoons flour
1/2 teaspoon salt
1 large can evaporated milk

Wash chili peppers—cut into strips or large pieces. Line casserole with layers of chili peppers. Cover with cheese and top with another layer of peppers. Beat eggs, flour, salt and milk; pour over cheese. Bake 45 minutes at 350° until custard sets.

Zucchini Cheese Custard

2 tablespoons butter

4 eggs

2 cups shredded Jack cheese with jalapenos

2 cups shredded cheddar cheese

1/2 cup bread crumbs

2 cloves garlic, minced or pressed

2 tablespoons grated onion

4 cups (about 4 medium sized) grated zucchini

1/3 cup grated Parmesan cheese

Coat the bottom and sides of shallow 2-quart baking dish with butter and set aside.

Beat eggs in large mixing bowl. Stir in Jack cheese with peppers, cheddar cheese, bread crumbs, garlic, and onion until well blended. Fold in zucchini. Scoop the mixture into buttered baking dish. Smooth top, then sprinkle with Parmesan cheese.

Bake uncovered, 350° until top is well browned and center is firm when lightly touched, about 45 minutes. Let cool 10 minutes before serving.

Serves 8 to 10.

Gallery Bookshop & Bookwinkles Childrens Books of Mendocino

Tony Miksak's
"Staff Meeting Frittata"

This easy-to-make egg dish serves up to 12 persons in small quantities, or 4 persons in large portions, and is a great Sunday breakfast with muffins and lattes. Use an oven-proof steel or cast iron skillet. For a large group, use eight eggs and a 13-15" skillet; for two to four persons, use four eggs and a 9" skillet.

Directions—

Egg mixture:

4-8 eggs
1/4 to 1/2 cup milk
1 crushed garlic clove
4 green onion tops, minced
pinch of oregano, marjoram, dill

Sauté:

1 large white onion
1 bunch asparagus (15 spears), tips only
10 white mushrooms
2 crushed garlic cloves
1 bunch spinach, well-washed, leaves only
**   (pre-packaged leaves save time)**
1/2 cup best parmesan cheese
1/2 teaspoon paprika

Beat eggs vigorously with milk. Add one crushed garlic clove and green onions. Rub in oregano, marjoram and dill. Set aside.

Cut vegetables into small bite-size chunks (not fine). Preheat oil in a cast iron or steel skillet with a metal or oven-proof handle. Add onions and sauté two minutes on medium heat. Add asparagus and mushrooms. Simmer until mushrooms are softened. Add garlic and spinach. When spinach has wilted, pour eggs over the top, stirring and shaking just enough to make sure eggs

104

reach the bottom of the pan. Lower heat. Sprinkle parmesan generously over the top; finish with a dusting of paprika.

When edges of frittata are well done and the middle is beginning to firm, place under a pre-heated broiler on high heat. Watch carefully. In a minute or three the frittata will puff up to twice its former height. When high points of top begin to brown, remove and serve immediately, directly from the skillet. Let guests see the gorgeous finished dish before cutting it out of the pan. The frittata will quickly lose its puffiness, but none of its flavor. This dish is excellent reheated next day; also excellent cold.

Variations:

Add any or all of the following in any order you like before pouring eggs over the top: cooked potatoes, bell peppers, chunks of hard cheese (blue cheese makes a great flavor surprise), marinated artichoke hearts, fresh peas or any cooked vegetable leftovers you may have handy.

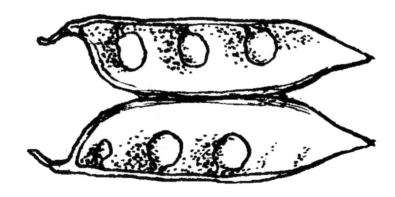

Sharoni's
Grits Soufflé

"I used to make this dish for my little girl's play group when it was our turn to host (she's now 17). Everyone loved it even if they usually despised grits. It has also made the rounds of countless potluck dinners over the years and is right at the top of my list of favorite 'comfort foods.' It's perfect with a fresh fruit or tossed green salad and some crusty bread."

- 4-1/2 cups water
- 1 teaspoon salt
- 2 teaspoons sugar
- 1 cup hominy grits (quick cooking)
- 4 ounces (1 stick) butter cut into pieces
- 4 eggs, slight beaten
- 1 to 2 tablespoons minced, dried roasted garlic, to taste,
  (or substitute minced fresh garlic to taste)
- Tabasco sauce, to taste
- 3 cups grated sharp cheddar cheese
- 1 teaspoon paprika, divided use
- 1/2 cup bread crumbs

Preheat oven to 350°. In a heavy 3-4 quart saucepan bring the water to boiling and add salt, sugar, and grits. Cook 3-5 minutes, stirring constantly. Remove saucepan from heat and add butter, eggs, garlic, Tabasco, cheese, and 112 teaspoon paprika. Stir well to blend thoroughly Taste mixture and adjust seasoning to taste, adding salt or pepper as desired. Pour into a 2-1/2 quart buttered baking dish and sprinkle with bread crumbs and remaining paprika. Bake uncovered for 1 hour or until bubbling and golden brown. Serve immediately.

Serves 8 to 10.

Desserts

The Old Milano Hotel of Gualala

Baked Apples A La Milano

Green baking apples

Wash apples and scoop out core with melon ball spoon. Place apples in foil-lined baking dish. Put small pat of butter in core of each apple. Put about 1 inch of water in bottom of dish and cover with foil. Bake at 350° until apples are soft enough to eat with spoon (45 minutes to 1 hour).

1 12-ounce package fresh or frozen cranberries

1/2 cup sweet butter

1 6-ounce can orange juice concentrate [no water]

3 cups brown sugar

3 teaspoons allspice

1/8 cup DeKuyper Orange Liquer

Cook all ingredients for sauce in double boiler until cranberries 'pop' or soften. Add sugar to taste.

Spoon sauce over baked apples. Garnish with walnuts, grated orange peel or mint.

110

Blackberry Inn of Mendocino

Mom Sjolund's Applesauce Cake

2 cups flour
2 teaspoons baking soda
3 tablespoons chocolate
1 cup sugar
1 large tablespoon cornstarch
1 teaspoon cinnamon
1/2 teaspoon cloves
1/2 teaspoon nutmeg
pinch of salt

In a large bowl, sift the above dry ingredients.

Then mix in the following:

3/4 cup chopped walnuts
3/4 cup raisins or chopped cooked prunes
1 3/4 cup applesauce
3/4 cup melted and cooled margarine

Mix well. Bake in greased 8 1/2"x8 1/2" glass baking dish for 1 hour and 10 minutes at 325°.

Joshua Grindle Inn of Mendocino

Arlene's Spicy Baked Pears with Yogurt

Winner 1989 California Summer Fruits award

Use largest pyrex dishes.

11 large ripe pears
1 cup dark brown sugar
1 1/2 cups orange juice
      (or enough to make 1/2 inch of liquid in baking dish)
1/4 cup butter
cinnamon
mace
pinch of ground cloves

vanilla yogurt

Line bottom of glass baking dish with the brown sugar. Sprinkle sugar layer generously with cinnamon, mace and pinch of cloves (if spices are sprinkled on top of pears, the cinnamon will burn). Slice pears in half, remove core and stem. Lay pears cut side down on sugar mixture. Dot with butter.

Next day: Pour orange juice over pears. Bake at 350° for 15-20 minutes or until pears are tender.

To serve, place pear cut side down in a serving dish, pour some of the brown sugar/orange juice mixture over the pear and top with a dollop of yogurt and freshly grated nutmeg.

C. O. Packard House Bed & Breakfast of Mendocino

Pear in Puff
(a là Packard House)

9 ounces fresh ready-made puff pastry

8 teaspoons light brown sugar

2 tablespoons butter (plus extra for brushing)

3 pears, peeled, halved & cored

vanilla yogurt, crème fraîche or vanilla ice cream (if it's for dessert)

On lightly floured surface, roll out dough. Cut out six rounds 4 inches in diameter.

Place the rounds on a large cookie sheet and chill for 30 minutes.

Cream together the brown sugar and butter in a small bowl.

Prick the pastry rounds all over with a fork and spread a little butter on each one.

Slice pear halves lenthwise, keeping the pears intact at the tip. Carefully fan out the slices slightly.

Place a fanned-out pear half on top of each dough round. Make small flutes around the edge of the dough rounds and generously brush each pear with melted butter.

Bake in preheated oven at 400° for 15-20 minutes, until pastry is well risen and golden in color. Serve warm with a little crème or yogurt.

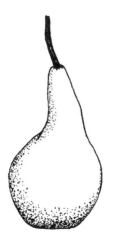

Corners of the Mouth of Mendocino

Osha's Tofu [Fruit or Squash] Pie

1 1/2 cup whole wheat pastry flour
2/3 cup butter
1/2 cup wheat germ or ground nuts
1/4 cup cold water

Pie Shell:
    Cut butter and flour together to pea size, add wheat germ, mix, and add water, form into ball. This is enough for 2 bottom shells or a top and bottom for fruit pies if desired.

Pie Filling:
    2 cups of fruit [berries or sliced peaches, etc.]
    or 2 cups cooked, peeled, drained squash [any kind]
    1/2 cup honey [maple syrup is nice with some fruit]
    1 cup [8 ounces] fresh tofu [smashed, creamed or blendered]
For Squash Filling:
    tablespoons oil or melted butter/margarine
    1/2 teasoon lemon extract
    1 tablespoon cinnamon
    a sprinkle of nutmeg on top
For Fruit Filling:
    1 teaspoon vanilla
    1/2 teaspoon cinnamon
    1 cup similar fruit-flavored yogurt
For either:
    a dash of salt
    1/4 cup diced walnuts or pecans for topping
Filling:
    Basically combine all ingredients (except nut or nutmeg toppings) and pour or spoon into pie shell. The fruit can be placed in pie shell and everything else combined and poured over. For the squash pie, blender everything together (you might need to add a bit of the squash cooking water) for a creamy 'pumpkin pie' consistency.
    Bake for 40 minutes at 375°.

The Seagull Inn of Mendocino

Bread and Butter Pudding with Blackberry Maple Sauce

Pudding:

>   1 pound loaf of day-old sweet French bread
>   1/4 pound real butter
>   3 eggs
>   2 cups heavy cream
>   1/3 cup sugar
>   1 tablespoon vanilla

Sauce:

>   3/4 cup maple syrup
>   2 cups fresh Mendocino blackberries
>   1 1/2 tablespoons blackberry brandy

Slice bread in 1/4-inch slices; butter each slice with room temperature butter. Place bread slices in a staggered line up in a 3 pound loaf pan.

Beat eggs, cream, sugar and vanilla until well-blended, pour over bread and bake at 325° for 30 to 40 minutes in water bath (insert bread pan in a 9"x13"x2" baking pan with 1/2-inch water).

Heat maple syrup to a boil in a 1 quart heavy-bottomed sauce pan. Reduce heat and simmer until reduced by half, 10 to 15 minutes. Stir with metal spoon. Add berries, simmer 5 minutes covered. Uncover pan, skim off any surface foam, then simmer uncovered until thickened slightly.

Add brandy, burn off alcohol, simmer 2 more minutes. Pour over pudding. Pudding can be served hot or at room temperature. Sauce should be served hot.

Desserts

Albion River Inn of Albion

Chef Stephen Smith's
Lemon-Ginger Crème Caramel
with Sautéed Strawberries & Black Currant Liqueur

Recipe can be cut in half with good results.

Custard:

  1 1/2 cups whipping cream

  1 cup whole milk

  2 cups granulated sugar for caramel sauce

  3/4 cup granulated sugar for custard

  1 vanilla bean or 1 tablespoon vanilla extract

  4 tablespoons fresh minced ginger

  2 lemons-zest & juice

  4 eggs, lightly beaten

  8 (4-6 ounce) ramekins or small coffee cups

  water bath with lid

Sautéed Strawberries:

  2 pints sliced fresh strawberries

  2 tablespoons granulated sugar

  4 ounces Crème de Cassis

  2 ounces sweet butter

Methods:

Caramel Sauce:
    Melt 2 cups granulated sugar on high heat until golden brown & clear. Divide into ramekins and cool 5 minutes.
Custard:
    In sauce pan combine first 6 ingredients and heat until hot—not boiling. Add eggs and whisk together. Strain into 8 ramekins and place in hot water bath with water level 1/2 way up their sides. Cover and bake at 350° until 'set,' about 45 minutes. Remove from water bath and refrigerate until cool,

about 3 hours. Can use foil to cover water bath. Vent so steam escapes and doesn't condense on custards. Custard will keep up to 3 days in refrigerator.

Strawberries:

Right before serving, melt 1 ounce sweet butter in sauté pan. Sauté strawberries on medium-high for 1 minute. Add Cassis, sugar, and reserved 1 ounce butter and swirl until melted. Divide among 8 dessert plates.

Presentation:

Loosen chilled custard from ramekin with thin blade, invert custard on center of prepared dessert plate and garnish with fresh mint.

Banana Rhubarb Wheel Upside-Down Cake

1/2 cup butter or margarine

3/4 cup brown sugar, packed

1/2 teaspoon ground cinnamon

1/4 teaspoon ground cloves

4 ripe bananas

2 stalks rhubarb

2 cups all purpose flour

2 teaspoons baking powder

1/2 teaspoon salt

4 eggs

1 1/2 cups sugar

1/2 cup milk

1/4 cup cream sherry

Set oven to 350°. Place butter, brown sugar, cinnamon, and cloves into oven-proof round skillet. Place over low heat, stirring occasionally until mixture bubbles. Remove from heat. Arrange cross-wise sliced banana and rhubarb slices in concentric circles atop butter/sugar mixture.

Sift flour with baking powder and salt. Break eggs into a 3 quart mixing bown, and beat with a rotary beater until thick and fluffy. Continue beating, adding sugar in three portions, until mixture is thick and spongy.

With wooden spoon or rubber spatula, cut and fold in flour mixture and liquids alternately, in three or four portions, ending with flour. When batter is smooth, pour over fruit and spread gently, leaving the rim slightly higher. Bake cake about 25 to 30 minutes, or until cake tests done with either a toothpick or a fingertip. Cool in skillet for about 5 minutes, then, placing serving plate on top of pan, invert onto serving plate. Serve warm.

Serves 6-8.

Whale Watch Inn By The Sea Bed & Breakfast of Gualala

Noodle Kugel

Beat together until smooth:

    3 eggs

    1 1/2 cups cottage cheese

    3/4 cup sour cream

    8 ounces cream cheese

    1 1/2 teaspoons vanilla

    2 teaspoons cinnamon

    1/2 cup honey

    dash of salt

Chop:

    8 ounces dried apricots

Boil **4 cups egg noodles** in lightly salted water until just tender. Drain, rinse, and butter.

Combine all ingredients and spread into a well-buttered casserole.

Top with a mixture of:

    1/2 cup bread crumbs

    2 teaspoons cinnamon

    1/2 cup brown sugar

Dot with butter. Bake uncovered 20-25 minutes in 375° oven. Serves 12 to 15.

Spring Ranch of Little River

Garden Pumpkin Pie

1 3/4 cups cooked, mashed pumpkin

2 fresh ranch brown eggs

1/2 cup brown sugar, firmly packed

1 1/2 teaspoon cinnamon

1/4 teaspoon ginger

1/4 teaspoon salt

1/4 teaspoon nutmeg

1 cup whole milk

Get a pumpkin from a pumpkin patch or your grocery store; a sugar pie pumpkin is best but most any pumpkin will make a good pie. Cut pumpkin into chunks, removing the seeds and insides. The chunks of pumpkin can be cooked in a pot on top of the stove or baked in a covered dish in the oven; put a little water in the bottom. Cooking takes about 45 minutes, or more. Cook until a fork will easily penetrate the pumpkin meat. Then peel the outside rind off each piece and either mash, put through a sieve or puree in a food processor.

Now for the pie:

Beat the 2 eggs until frothy. Add the sugar gradually to the eggs. Add the spices and salt. Gradually add the milk and then the pumpkin.

Pour mixture into an unbaked 9-inch pie shell.

Bake at 450° for 10 minutes; then reduce to 350° for 30 to 35 minutes.

The Mendocino Ice Cream Company of Mendocino

Pumpkin Ice Cream

16 ounces pumpkin, fresh or canned, pureed
1 cup brown sugar, firmly packed
1/4 teaspoon cinnamon, ground
1/8 teaspoon nutmeg, ground
1/4 teaspoon ginger, ground
1 cup half-and-half
1/2 teaspoon orange peel, grated
1/4 cup orange juice
2 cups whipping cream

Combine all ingredients in a large bowl. Stir enough to mix evenly. Pour into an electric or hand crank ice cream freezer and freeze according to manufacturer's directions. Be sure to let the kids (of any age) lick the beaters when you pull them out of the freezer. This recipe makes about two quarts and may be doubled for larger freezers.

The Ravens Restaurant at The Stanford Inn by the Sea of Mendocino

Wild Huckelberry Sorbet with Lavender Wafers

Sorbet:

1 pint wild Huckelberries

2 cups water

1 1/2 cup sugar

1 lemon-zested, juiced

Combine all ingredients, except lemon zest, in a sauce pan. Bring to boil, reduce heat and simmer 10 minutes. Cool, add zest, and puree mixture. Place in a suitable container for freezing, such as a metal bowl or baking dish. Freeze to 'slush' and whisk briskly. Return to freezer until firm, or freeze in an ice cream maker.

Serve with Lavender Wafers.

Wafers:

1/2 cup soft butter

1/2 cup cugar

1/2 cup all purpose flour

pinch of salt

2 egg whites

1/4 cup dried Lavender blossoms

Preheat oven to 375°. Grease cookie sheet.

Cream butter and sugar, mix in flour and salt, then egg whites to form a smooth batter.

Drop tablespoons full of batter evenly spaced on cookie sheet. With the back of a spoon dipped in water, spread each into a thin circle.

Sprinkle with Lavender blossoms and bake 6-8 minutes or until edges turn golden. Remove with spatula while still hot.

Cool and serve with sorbet.

Serves six.

Reeves' Garden Cottage of Mendocino

Nut Torte

2 cups hazel nuts or almonds,
       ground in a nut grinder or chopped in a Cuisinart
3/4 cup sugar
7 eggs
1/2 pint whipping cream

Beat eggs, add sugar gradually. Beat these ingredients until creamy, several minutes.

Fold ground nuts carefully into the batter.

Bake in a greased 9" round pan with a removable rim.

Put in a cold oven and bake 25 to 30 minutes at 350°. Test with a thin knitting needle in the center. When the needle comes out clean, the cake is done.

Serve with whipped cream, flavored with a little sugar and vanilla, and fresh berries or cranberry sauce.

If preferred the cold cake can be covered with the whipped cream and decorated with some nuts.

The Roadhouse of Elk

Devilsfood Cake

12 ounces cocoa
4 ounces oil
1/2 cup milk
1 cup brown sugar
1 egg yolk

Cook and stir above ingedients in a double boiler over hot water. Remove from heat when thickened.

2 1/4 cups cake flour
1 teaspoon soda
1/2 teaspoon salt
1 cup white sugar
1/2 cup butter
2 egg yolks
1/4 cup water
1/2 cup milk
1 teaspoon vanilla
2 egg whites

Sift cake flour before measuring. Resift with soda and salt.

Sift white sugar. Beat butter until soft and add sugar slowly. Blend until light and creamy. Beat in one at a time the egg yolks. Add flour, soda, salt mixture to butter mixture in three parts, alternating with thirds of water, milk and vanilla. Stir batter until smooth after each addition. Stir in chocolate mixture.

Whip egg whites until stiff but not dry. Fold them lightly into the cake batter. Bake in 2 greased 9-inch round layer pans for about 35 minutes at 350° (Watch baking time-this varies, sometimes more, sometimes less).

Frosting:

>**1 cup milk**
>
>**1/2 cup flour**
>
>**1/4 teaspoon salt**
>
>**1 cup sugar**
>
>**1/2 cup butter**
>
>**1/2 cup shortening**
>
>**2 teaspoons vanilla**

Cook milk, flour and salt over medium heat. Stir until very thick. Let cool.

Beat sugar, butter and shortening until smooth and creamy. Add to this the cooled mixture. Add vanilla, beat again and frost cake.

Victorian Farmhouse of Little River

Carole Molnar's
Chocolate Chip Date Cake

Place 1 cup chopped dates in a bowl with 1 teaspoon baking soda. Pour 1 1/2 cups boiling water over dates. Let sit about 10 minutes.

In another bowl cream together 1/2 cup shortening with 1 cup sugar and 2 eggs.

Pour date mixture over shortening, sugar and egg mixture. Add 1 1/2 cups flour and 3/4 teaspoon baking powder. Pour into greased and floured 9"x13" pan.

Top with a mixture of 1 small package chocolate chips, 1/2 cup nuts and 1/2 cup sugar. Bake at 350° for 1/2 hour.

North Coast Brewing Company of Fort Bragg

Mendocino Chocolate Mud Cake

1 1/2 cups flour

1 1/4 cups sugar

3/4 cup cocoa

2 cups milk

1 1/8 cups chopped walnuts

3/4 teaspoon salt

3 teaspoons baking powder

1 1/2 tablespoons vanilla

1 ounce melted butter

1/2 cup Old Number 38 Stout beer

1/2 pound brown sugar

1/3 cup cocoa

Preheat oven to 350° F. In large mixing bowl, mix together flour, 1 1/2 cups sugar, 3/4 cup cocoa, milk, and 1 1/8 cups chopped walnuts. Pour into oblong baking pan approximately 9" x 13".

In medium mixing bowl, mix together salt, baking powder, vanilla and melted butter. Stir into mixture in pan.

In small bowl, mix together Old # 38 Stout beer, brown sugar, and 1/3 cup cocoa. Gently stir into mixture in pan.

Bake at 350° for 35 minutes.

Country Inn of Fort Bragg

Chocolate Ribbon Cake

2 sticks butter or margarine

1 1/2 cups sugar

3 cups flour

1 1/2 teaspoon baking powder

1 1/2 teaspoon baking soda

1 1/2 teaspoon vanilla extract

12-ounce container sour cream

3 eggs

1/2 teaspoon ground cinnamon (optional)

3 squares semi-sweet chocolate, grated

Preheat oven to 350°. Grease and flour 9"x5" loaf pan or bundt pan. In large bowl with mixer at Medium speed, beat butter/margarine and sugar until light and fluffy. Reduce speed to Low; add flour, baking powder, baking soda, vanilla extract, sour cream and eggs; beat just until blended, occasionally scraping bowl with rubber spatula. Increase speed to Medium, beat 1 minute, occasionally scraping bowl with spatula.

Spread half of batter evenly in pan; sprinkle with half of grated chocolate and half of cinnamon (1/4 teaspoon); repeat with remaining batter, grated chocolate and cinnamon. Draw knife through batter a few times to swirl chocolate.

Bake cake 1 hour or until toothpick inserted in center comes out clean. Cool cake in pan on wire rack 10 minutes. Serve warm. Or cool cake completely on wire rack and serve later.

Greenwood Pier Inn of Elk

Chocolate Chip-Pecan Pie

Crust:

> **1 1/2 cups flour**
>
> **1/4 cup cold butter**
>
> **a sprinkle of salt**
>
> **2 tablespoons water**
>
> **1 egg**

Filling:

> **1/2 cup chocolate chips**
>
> **1 1/2 cups pecans**
>
> **1/2 cup brown sugar**
>
> **2 eggs**
>
> **1 teaspoon vanilla**
>
> **1 cup dark corn syrup**
>
> **1/2 cup butter**

Mix crust and roll out, placing it in a greased pie plate. Put chips on unbaked crust, then pecans.

Mix butter, eggs, sugar, vanilla till smooth, then add syrup. Pour over pecans and chips, then bake at 350° for 1 hour until solid.

Ackerman's Fine Foods of Mendocino

White Chocolate Amarreto Bundt Cake

    1 pound butter, at room temperature
    8 eggs
    2 cups sour cream
    2 tablespoons vanilla
    2 tablespoons brandy

Beat above ingredients until totally combined and smooth.

    4 cups sugar
    1 teaspoon salt
    1 teaspoon baking soda
    1 teaspoon nutmeg
    6 cups flour
    4 cups white chocolate chips
    2 ounces or more Amarreto

Add each ingredient—except Amaretto—and beat into batter until combined.

Pour batter in large bundt pan 3/4 full.

Bake at 350° for 1 hour and 10 minutes (test at one hour).

Let cake cool for 15 minutes, then flip out of pan.

Drizzle Amaretto over top.

Use remaining batter in muffin tins for individual cakes. Only bake for 45 minutes, though.

Desserts

Mendocino Soda Pop Company of Fort Bragg

Mendocino Root Beer Cake

1 1/3 cups Mendocino Root Beer (It's made with yeast)
 teaspoon root beer extract
1 white cake mix
2 tablespoons oil
3 egg whites

Mix all ingredients and beat 2 minutes.
Bake in 9" x 13" pan at 350° for 32 to 35 minutes.
Serve with whipped cream.

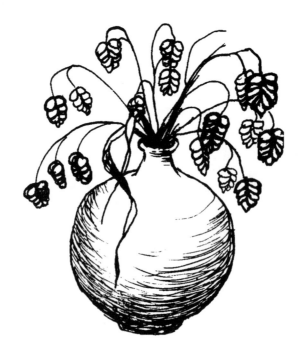

Brownies
&
Cookies

Mendocino Cookie Company of Mendocino & Fort Bragg

Scholkolade
[A Chocoholic's Dream Come True]

2 4-ounce bars German chocolate
1 tablespoon butter or margarine
2 eggs
3/4 cup sugar
1/4 cup flour
1/4 teaspoon baking powder
1/4 teaspoon cinnamon
1/8 teaspoon salt
1/2 teaspoon vanilla

Melt chocolate and butter over hot water. Cool.

Beat eggs until foamy, add sugar, 2 tablespoons at a time. Beat until thickened, 5 minutes on medium speed in mixer/blender. Blend in chocolate, add flour, baking powder, cinnamon, salt and blend. Add vanilla. Drop, by teaspoons, onto greased baking sheet. Bake at 350° for 8 to 10 minutes.

Brownies & Cookies

Cafe Beaujolais of Mendocino

Margaret Fox's
Chocolate Truffles

1 tablespoon instant coffee, dissolved in 1/4 cup water

8 ounces semi-sweet chocolate

1 ounce bitter chocolate

3 egg yolks

1/2 cup unsalted butter, cut into teaspoon-sized pieces

1/4 cup Myer's rum or Grand Marnier

1/2 cup unsweetened cocoa

1/4 cup powdered sugar

Place coffee and both chocolates in the top of a double boiler, and stir with a whisk over medium heat until chocolate has melted. In a separate bowl, beat the egg yolks and add 1/2 cup of the chocolate mixture to them. Beat well and add back to the chocolate in the pan. Beat well for 2 minutes, cool 5 minutes, then gradually beat in the butter, one piece at a time. Be sure NO butter is visible, then add the rum or Grand Marnier.

Refrigerate about 1 1/2 hours, until firm enough to form truffles. Use either a pastry tube with a #7 point, or drop from a teaspoon onto a cookie sheet. Just make blobs on the cookie sheet—don't worry about appearance at this point. Re-refrigerate for at least half an hour.

Remove truffles from refrigerator. Combine cocoa and powdered sugar, and place in a container with a lid. Drop truffles into the cocoa mix and shake to coat them. Quickly roll into balls with your hands; the truffles can be irregular in shape. Store in a tightly covered container. Store in refrigerator.

Agate Cove Inn of Mendocino

Chocolate Walnut Cranberry Expresso Biscotti

2 cups unbleached all-purpose flour

1 cup white sugar

1/2 teaspoon baking powder

1/2 teaspoon soda

1/2 teaspoon salt

1/2 teaspoon cinnamon

1/4 teaspoon ground cloves

1/4 cup plus 1 tablesoon strong coffee (cooled)

1 tablespoon plus I teaspoon milk

1 large egg

1 teaspoon vanilla

3/4 cup walnuts

1 1/4 cup chocolate chips (semi-sweet)

3/4 cup dried cranberries or cherries

In a large mixing bowl, combine all dry ingredients and blend well.

In a small bowl, whisk together all liquids, add to dry ingredients with mixer. You may want to add a few drops of coffee to get mixture gooey.

Add chocolate chips, walnuts and cranberries. Turn dough out onto a well-floured board and form into 1/2" x 3 1/2" flat logs—cook on greased/floured cookie sheet at 350° for 20-25 minutes. Cook until cake-like. Cool.

Cut logs into 1/2" pieces, lay (cut-side down) fiat on cookie sheet and bake another 6-8 minutes at 300°—One side only. Cool and serve.

For a harder biscotti, cook both sides of cut pieces for 6-8 minutes each side.

Makes approximately 32 biscotti. Recipe easily doubles if needed.

Variations: Pistachios; almonds; dried cherries.

Reed Manor of Mendocino

Orange Candy Cookies

1/2 cup butter, melted

2 cups brown sugar, firmly packed

4 eggs, beaten

2 cups all purpose flour

1 pound orange candy slices, finely chopped

1 cup pecans, chopped

1 cup powdered sugar

Combine butter and brown sugar in large bowl; stir in eggs, mixing well.
Add flour, chopped orange candy, and pecans. Stir until well blended.
Pour into well greased jelly roll pan 15"x10"x1".
Bake at 350° for 25 minutes—Cool 15 minutes in pan.
Cut into 2"x2" squares—Cool completely in pan.
Remove squares from pan; cut in half diagonally.
Roll in powdered sugar.
Yields 6 dozen.

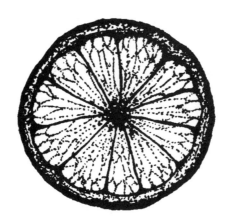

Mary's Country Kitchen of Gualala

Pat Adshade's
Oatmeal Crisp Cookies

2 cubes butter (1/2 pound)

2 cups granulated sugar

2 eggs

1 teaspoon vanilla

2 cups unsifted flour

1 teaspoon salt

1 teaspoon baking powder

1 teaspoon baking soda

2 1/2 cups rice krispies

1 1/2 cups oatmeal

1-6 ounce package chocolate chips

1/2 cup chopped nuts

1/2 cup raisins

In a large bowl cream butter, sugar, eggs, and vanilla. Add flour, salt, baking powder, and baking soda to well creamed butter mixture. Add remaining ingredients to the flour mixture. Stir in rice krispies last, very gently, so not to crush them.

Spray a cookie sheet with Pam. Drop mounded teaspoonful on cookie sheet. Dip a fork in water and flatten each mound of dough. The glob of dough should be at least as big as a pingpong ball. They do spread out as they bake.

Bake at 375° for 15-20 minutes or until light brown.

Yields about 5 dozen.

Have a glass of milk handy!

Mendocino Cookie Company of Mendocino & Fort Bragg

Beverlee Younger's
Amaretto Delights

1/2 cup egg whites (3 eggs)
1 1/4 cup sugar
/4 teaspoon salt
1/3 cup Amaretto liqueur
3 1/4 ounces coconut, flaked
4 ounces almonds, finely chopped

Beat egg whites until stiff. Gradually beat in sugar, one tablespoon at a time, until stiff and glossy. Add salt. Slowly beat in Amaretto. Fold in coconut and almonds.

Foil line cookie sheets. Drop heaping teaspoons on to foil. Bake at 325° for 20 minutes. Cool cookies on foil.

Store in air-tight container. Makes 4 dozen.

This is an Italian-style cookie, perfect for espresso drinks.

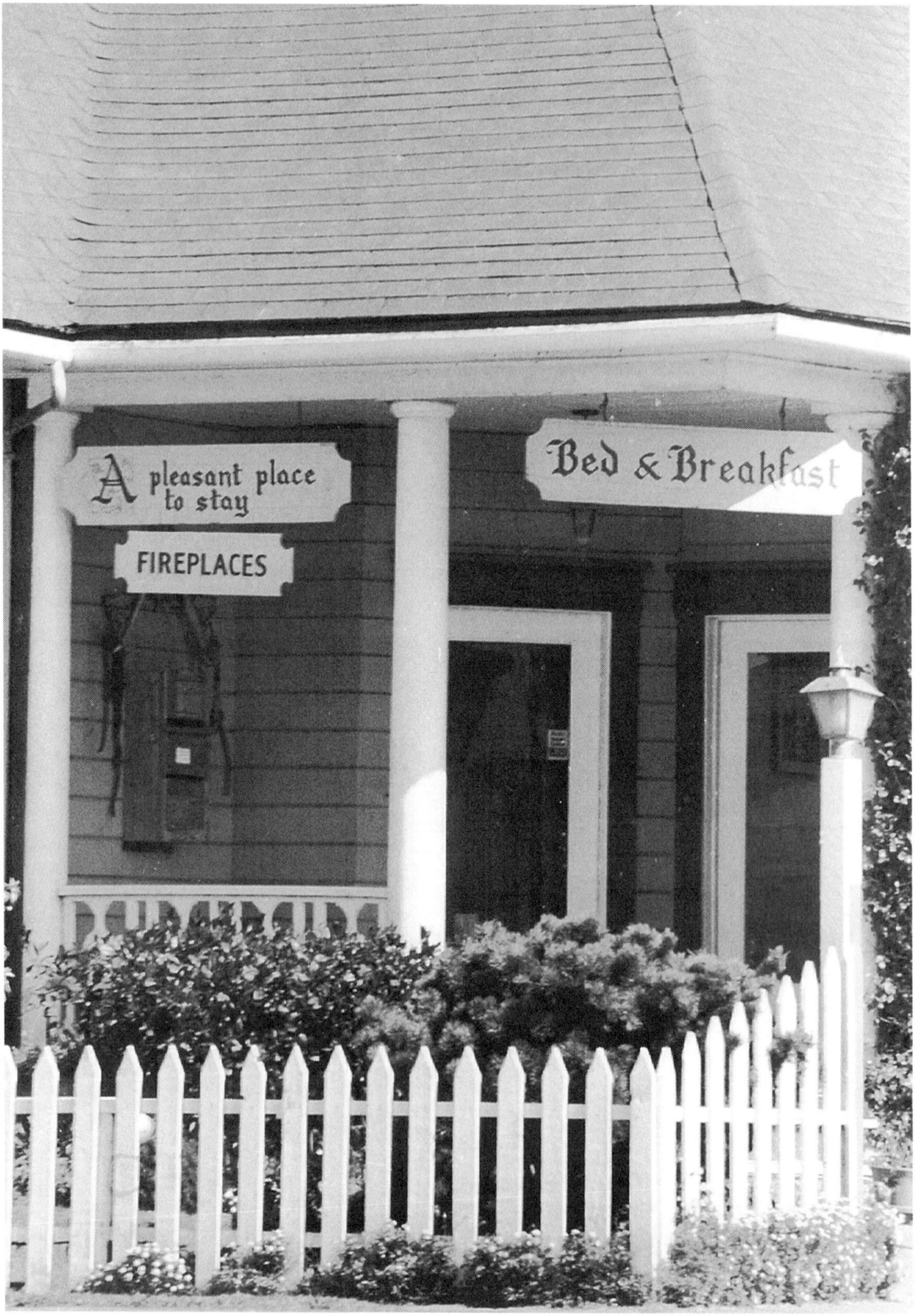
A pleasant place to stay
FIREPLACES
Bed & Breakfast

Contributors & Addresses

Ackerman's Fine Foods, 890 N. Franklin, Fort Bragg—961-1359
Agate Cove Inn, 11201 N. Lansing, Box 1150, Mendocino—937-0551/800-527-3111
Albion River Inn 3790 N. Hwy 1, Box 100, Albion—937-1919/800-479-7944
Anchor Bay Village Market, 35513 S. Hwy 1, Gualala—884-4245
Bay View Cafe, 45040 Main, Mendocino—937-4197
Blackberry Inn, 44951 Larkin Rd., Mendocino—937-5281
The Blue Heron Inn, 390 Kasten, Box 1142, Mendocino—937-4323
The Blue Victorian Inn & Antique Shop, 38911 N. Hwy. 1, Westport—964-6310
The Book Loft, 338 N. Main, Fort Bragg—964-0890
C. O. Packard House, 45170 Little Lake, Mendocino—937-2677
Cafe Beaujolais, 961 Ukiah, Box 1236, Mendocino—937-5614
Cafe Prima, 124 Laurel, Fort Bragg—964-0563
Café Vienna, 120 S. Main, Fort Bragg—964-8674
The Caspar Inn and Blues Cafe, 14961 Caspar Rd., Caspar—964-5565/964-9034
Caspar Institute, Box 88, Caspar
Chef for Hire, Chef Judith Henderson—962-0433
Cleone Lodge Inn, 24600 N. Hwy 101, Fort Bragg—964-2788/800-400-2189
Corners of the Mouth, 45105 Ukiah, Mendocino—937-5345
Country Inn, 632 N. Main, Fort Bragg—964-3737
The Courtyard, Main St., Box 148, Mendocino—937-0917
Cultured Affair Cafe, Corner Kasten & Albion—Mendocino, 937-1430
David's Delicatessen, 450 S. Franklin, Fort Bragg—964-1946
Drummond Farms, Box 1694, Mendocino—937-1758/800-924-5400—
Elk Cove Inn, 6300 S. Hwy 1, Elk—877-3321/800-275-2967
Fetzer Vineyards Tasting Room, 45070 Main, P.O. Box 144, Mendocino
        —937-6191/800-860-3347
The Food Company, Hwy 1 & Robinson Reef Rd. Gualala—884-1800
Fuller's Fine Herbs, Box 1344, Mendocino, Ca. 95460—937-0860—fuller4h@mcn.org
Gallery Bookshop & Bookwinkle's Children's Books, Main & Kasten, Mendocino
        —937-BOOK (2665)
The General Store, 301 "G" N. Main, Fort Bragg—961-1004
Glass Beach Inn, 726 N. Main, Fort Bragg—964-6774
Good Thyme Herb Co., P.O. Box 975, Mendocino, CA. 95460—964-0509
Greenwood Lodge Cottages, Box 196, Elk
Greenwood Pier Inn & Cafe, 5926 S. Hwy 1, Box 336, Elk—877-9997
Grey Whale Inn, 615 N. Main, Fort Bragg—964-0640/800-382-7244
The Harbor House Inn, 5600 S. Highway 1, Box 369, Elk—877-3203/800-720-7474
Harvest Market, Boatyard Center, Hwys 20 & 1, Fort Bragg—964-7000
Headlands Coffee House, 120 E. Laurel, Fort Bragg—964-1987
Heritage House, 5200 N. Hwy 1, Little River—937-5885/800-235-5885,
Howard Creek Ranch Inn, Box 121, Westport—964-6725
The Inn at Schoolhouse Creek, 7051 N. Hwy 1, Little River—937-5525/800-731-5525
John Dougherty House, 571 Ukiah St., Mendocino—937-5266/800-486-2104
Joshua Grindle Inn, 44800 Little Lake, Box 647, Mendocino—937-4143/800-GRINDLE
The Larkin Cottage, 44950 Larkin Rd., Mendocino—937-2567
Little River Inn, 7751 Hwy 1, Little River—937-5942/888-466-5683
Little River Restaurant, 7750 N. Hwy 1, Little River—937-4945

The MacCallum House Restaurant and Grey Whale Bar & Cafe, Albion St. Box 1317,
    Mendocino—937-5763/800-609-0492
Mary's Country Kitchen 38820 S. Hwy 1, Box 589, Gualala—884-3534
The Melting Pot, Corner Main & Lansing, Mendocino—937-0173
The Mendocino Cookie Company, 10450 Lansing, Mendocino—937-4843
    & The Company Store, 303 N. Main, Fort Bragg—964-0282
Mendocino Farmers' Market—937-2728
Mendocino Gift Company, 321 Kasten, Mendocino—937-5298
The Mendocino Ice Cream Company, 45090 Main, Mendocino—937-5884
Mendocino Mineral Water, 10689 Docker Hill Rd, Comptche—937-0547
Mendocino Mushrooms, Box 899, Mendocino—964-1646
Mendocino Mustard, 1260 N. Main, Fort Bragg—964-2250/800-964-2270
Mendocino Sea Vegetable Co., Box 1265, Mendocino—937-2050
Mendocino Soda Pop Company, Fort Bragg—961-1442
Mendocino Village Inn, 44860 Main, Box 636, Mendocino—937-0246/800-882-7029
Mendosa's, 10501 Lansing, Mendocino—937-5879
Moore Used Books, 990A Main, Mendocino—937-1537—cmoore@mcn.org
The Moosse Café, 390 Kasten, Mendocino—937-4323
North Coast Brewing Company, 444 N. Main, Fort Bragg—964-3400
North Coast Country Inn, 34591 S. Hwy 1, Gualala—884-4537/800-959-4537
The Nye Ranch, 23300 N. Hwy 1, Fort Bragg—964-0939
The Old Milano Hotel, 38300 S. Hwy 1, Gualala—884-3256
Old Stewart House Inn, 511 Stewart, Fort Bragg—961-0775
Pacific Star Winery, 33000 N. Hwy 1, Fort Bragg—964-1155
Platt House, 19100 Neptune, Fort Bragg—961-9676
Pot Gourmet, 10481 Lansing, Mendocino—937-3663
The Pudding Creek Inn, 700 N. Main, Fort Bragg—964-9529/800-227-9529
The Ravens Restaurant at The Stanford Inn by the Sea , Coast Hwy 1
    & Comptche-Ukiah Road, P.O. Box 487, Mendocino—937-5615/800-331-8884
Reeves' Garden Cottage, 511 Ukiah, Mendocino—937-5686
The Restaurant, 418 N. Main, Fort Bragg—964-9800
Reed Manor, Pallet Drive, Box 127, Mendocino—937-5446
The Roadhouse Cafe, S. Highway 1, Elk—877-3285
Round Man's Smokehouse, 137 Laurel, Fort Bragg—964-5954
Sai Poma Ranch, Box 193, Comptche
Sea Gull Inn, 44594 Albion, Box 317, Mendocino—937-5204/888-937-5204
Sea Rock Inn Bed & Breakfast, 11101 Lansing, Box 906, Mendocino
    —937-0926/800-906-0926
Serenisea Ocean Cabins, 36100 S. Highway 1, Gualala—884-3836/800-331-3836
Sharon Robinson's Wedding Cakes & Wonderful Desserts, Box 1118, Mendocino—962-0384
Spring Ranch, 8501 N. Hwy 1, Little River
St. Orres Restaurant, 36601 Highway 1, Box 523, Gualala—884-3303
Stevenswood Lodge, 8211 N. Hwy 1, Little River—937-2810/800-421-2810
Victorian Farmhouse, 7001 N. Hwy 1, Little River, P.O. Box 661, Mendocino—937-0697
Well House West, 311 N. Franklin, Fort Bragg—964-2101
Weller House Inn, 524 Stewart, Ft. Bragg—964-4415/877-8WELLER
Whale Watch Inn By The Sea Bread & Breakfast, 35100 S. Hwy 1, Gualala—884-3667
Whitegate Inn, 499 Howard, Box 150, Mendocino—937-4892/800-531-7282
Wine World at Anchor Bay Village Market, 35513 S. Hwy 1, Gualala—884-4245
The Wool Loft Bed & Breakfast, 32751, Navarro Ridge Rd., Albion—937-0377

Index of Recipes